The Nimble Company

**A Proactive, Socially Responsible Framework
for Driving Sustained Profits and Growth
in a Chronically Chaotic World.**

Excerpt rights granted and use encouraged with the following credit: "From *The Nimble Company: A Proactive, Socially Responsible Framework for Driving Sustained Profits and Growth in a Chronically Chaotic World* by Dr. David Gruder and Mark S.A. Smith. Get details at NimbilityWorks.com/media"

For other reprint rights, contact MS@NimbilityWorks.com or contact@DrGruder.com

Published by NimbilityWorks Media™
NimbilityWorks.com/media

v1.01

ISBN 978-1-884059-67-4 Paperback
ISBN 978-1-884059-68-1 Hardback

Printed in the United States of America.

The Nimble Company

**A Proactive, Socially Responsible Framework
for Driving Sustained Profits and Growth
in a Chronically Chaotic World.**

Amid perpetual upheavals and accelerating world changes, we transition from the Experience Economy where buyers choose *memorable* outcomes to the Transformational Economy where buyers choose *meaningful, authentic,* and socially responsible outcomes.

Because your customers want to become a better version of themselves, your company must become a better version of itself.

This book's premise: the future belongs to the nimble, those able to resiliently innovate to deliver meaningful goods and services that customers seek. Being nimble makes demands on your company that go beyond traditional business strategies, tactics, and company culture.

This book takes a fresh look at the root causes of upheavals and offers pragmatic solutions that can address these causes in today's chronically volatile business environment.

Dr. David Gruder and Mark S A Smith

Early Praise

"Only once in a great while do words hold tremendous power to invoke significant change. The authors, Dr. David Gruder and Mark S.A. Smith have collaborated to create a foundation for leadership in a world where the rate of change has become so exponential that it calls for an entirely new perspective in leadership. To say that we are in a transformational phase of human evolution would be an understatement, and this set of books sets the path forward in a way never before attempted at such a grand scale. We will include copies of these books in every HR package, not just for the executives."
– Mark Hewitt, Founder, **NuGen Development** & **The Lydian Foundation**

"I could not put down The Nimble Company. Mark and David really know what they are talking about. When I finished the book, I had more pages of actionable ideas than any other business book I have read in the last decade. I have ordered a copy for all of our people. Learn from this and implement it. Your success depends on it."
– Frank Candy, Founder and President, **American Speakers Bureau Corporation**

"This book is a meaty masterpiece on how businesses must operate to thrive today, why they don't, and how to fix yours so it does. It includes the full range of concepts and tools for making sense of chaos, extracting conviction from uncertainty, and seizing opportunity out of disruption. Having founded and led a company for over two decades, this is the first book I've read that hits execution risk head on and gives me the full range of tools to help my company and others thrive in change. Every one of my clients will have a copy on their desk on Day One. Indispensable!"

– Mark DiMassimo, Founder and Creative Chief, **DiGo**

"This guide to agile governance is a must-have for every executive. Organized in crystal-clear, user-friendly format, it shows how blindspots are avoided through inclusiveness. Park your ego at the door and keep this book at your side."

– Douglas Mulhall, Author of *Our Molecular Future*, former founding CEO of **ICTV**, and Cofounder of **Elastrin Therapeutics**

Disclaimer

Neither the authors nor the publisher assume any responsibility for errors, inaccuracies, or omissions. Any slights of people or organizations are unintentional.

This publication is not intended for use as a source of psychological, security, technical, legal, accounting, financial, or other professional advice. If you need advice concerning these matters, consult a qualified professional as this is not a substitute for professional counsel.

Neither the authors nor the publisher accept any responsibility or liability for your use of the ideas presented herein. Conversely, neither the publisher nor authors will lay claim to any profits you make based on the principles, mindsets, and tactics this book provides.

Some suggestions concerning business practices may inadvertently introduce practices deemed unlawful in certain professions, states, municipalities, countries. You should be aware of the various laws governing your business practices in your industry and in your location.

While the websites referenced were personally reviewed by the authors, we can make no guarantees as to their safety. Practice safe Internet surfing with current antivirus software and a browser with robust security settings.

Contents

The Nimble Company

A Proactive, Socially Responsible Framework for Driving Sustained Profits and Growth in a Chronically Chaotic World.

Chapter 1:
Constant Upheavals – The Big
Corporate Challenge

Raphael was on his way to meet with his executive coach, Sabrina.[1] She always seemed to provide just the right perspective to help him navigate the challenges he faced as the company CEO. And today was no different. He needed some insight. He spotted her in line as he walked into the café.

"Hi Sabrina!" he waved at her. "Let me get that for you."

"Raphael! I'm so glad to see you." she smiled genuinely. "Sure, I gratefully accept your generosity."

They picked up their drinks and headed to a corner table.

"How *are* you?" Sabrina asked. Raphael knew why she earnestly asked that question when they first met. She's checking on my mindset, he thought.

"Happy, healthy, and challenged," he smiled.

"I'm glad for all of that," she said with a hint of irony in her voice. "Why are you happy?"

---

[1] This is a follow-on conversation that started in the companion book, *The Nimble C-Suite*.

Raphael chuckled, "I knew you'd start there! *The Nimble C-Suite* book you recommended really opened my eyes. There were so many insights that expanded my perspective. I didn't know how much I didn't know about understanding the economic changes driven by customers insisting on social responsibility. I'm happy because I have a bead on what to do to shift my executive team to being nimble and it's beginning to work."

"What you've just learned wasn't taught when you were in B-school, so it's no surprise that you're experiencing growth. Give yourself credit for searching for new answers to new questions and applying what you've learned. Good job! What's the challenge?"

"I now understand that being nimble means increasing resilience and innovation and the opposite of being nimble is brittle, where change breaks things. Yet there are so many problems, the book called them upheavals, that I don't know where to start managing execution risk to increase our resilience" Raphael shared.

"What's top of mind for you?" queried Sabrina. She sure knows how to tap into my motivation, Raphael observed.

"Right now, it's finding and hiring good people. We can't grow without a bigger team and my HR department struggles to find well-qualified candidates. People seem to jump companies for just a few dollars more and those on the market want the sun, moon, and stars for even an entry-level position."

"An all-too-common challenge. What else?" Raphael observed that Sabrina would first get all the issues on the table before discussing solutions.

"We're trying to get a handle on all of the risk factors we need to think about as we move forward. With a socially responsible company, there seem to be more than in the past. And I need my team to develop plans to be resilient. A catastrophe shut down one of my competitors for two weeks. They may not make it. I can't let that happen to my company." Raphael reflected that it seemed like a tall order.

"There are more risk factors than ever, and although technology has solved some challenges its also introduced new ones. What have you done to identify your execution risks?"

"I've asked my exec team to list what they see as potential execution risks. I've told them to be as thorough as possible and to let go of any concerns about discussing elements that might impact their career. They're a bit worried that their list will reveal that they aren't up to the job. Having them not tell me the whole story concerns me because it creates a blindspot in my leadership." Raphael was genuinely concerned.

"Why do you think that is?" Sabrina said thoughtfully.

"I have a seasoned team with experience in our industry. Most come from other companies where there was rapid chastisement for not doing the job fast enough or a demotion if a disaster happening on their watch. I guess they have PTSD." Raphael laughed at his insight.

"So, your team carries bad culture residue from their past positions. Could this be the root cause of your challenges, including your finding-good-people problem?"

"You're right! Hmmm… I'm not sure how to fix that." Raphael said hesitantly.

"May I offer you a perspective?" Sabrina seemed to always ask before she offered insight. I need to do that with my team, thought Raphael. It feels less like direction and more like discovery; that could lessen resistance to new ideas.

"Please do!"

"There are three reasons why upheavals happen: blind spots, misunderstandings, and withholds. You must first clear these from your culture if you're going to identify all sources of execution risk, which manifest as upheavals."

"Makes sense and seems so simple. Yet how do I do that?" wondered Raphael.

"There's another book in the Nimbility series you need to read next..."

You hold in your hand that book.

The Core Issue That Limits a Company's Nimbility

The number one cause of business problems: the common executive structure and mixing of strategic and tactical roles in the *C-Suite*.[2]

This book is the companion to *The Nimble C-Suite: How to Align the Diverse Strengths of Your Executive Team to Predictably Deliver Extraordinary Outcomes in a Transformational Economy,* which dives into the first priority for a Nimble Company: forming a nimble C-Suite.

------

[2] We define C-Suite for the purposes of this book as the executive team who are individually accountable and responsible for key business functions in the organization, traditionally recognized by the word *Chief* in their title.

In that book we describe the critical missing role in the C-Suite and reorganize it to psychologically align with temperament best suited to the role. Right matching temperament – how one views the world – to a role, allows one to function within their *zone of genius*, operating in flow and with little, if any, internal friction.

When the C-Suite mixes strategic roles – necessarily focused on long-term initiatives and goals, with tactical roles – necessarily focused on short-term initiatives and goals, the resulting tension creates high friction and triggers unnecessary upheavals. We solve this issue by splitting the C-Suite into a strategically focused *S-Suite* and a tactically focused *T-Suite* to better align worldviews and execution time frames.

This book continues the Nimbility conversation by focusing on causes of upheavals, how to spot them, how to prevent them, and how to navigate them when they happen.

The Central Idea: Nimbility

Everything you'll read and consider in this book centers on bringing *Nimbility* to your organization.

Nimbility is the combination of high resilience and high innovation that are necessary attributes for profiting from upheavals. See Figure 1.

High Resilience

| Bored | | Nimble |

Low Innovation ———————————|——————————— **High Innovation**

| Stagnant | | Oppositional |

Low Resilience

Figure 1: The Nimbility Matrix — Mapping Resilience against Innovation Determines Your Nimbility Level

Innovation is the capacity to increase the desirability, utility, and value of a product, whether it's goods or services. *Resilience* is the ability to rapidly recover from necessary changes, stress, and unplanned impacts.

The obvious value of innovation is competitive performance, protecting and increasing profit margins, and corporate sustainability in a changing market. It's also way more fun. Innovation is set by culture and team rewards for looking for better ways to bring more value to the team, customers, stakeholders, and the planet.

A key value of resilience is risk reduction because it allows rapid recovery from an undesired state, reducing the cost of risk, and therefore contributing to lowered risk. Resilience is set by systems and policies that can quickly respond to change, with the necessary resources to absorb shocks and quickly recover.

Nimbility is inherently lower risk, much lower than other options, making conventional risk-taking and innovation much safer from a career and corporate perspective.

We apply the Nimbility Matrix to both your organization and the individuals involved when assessing a situation. For your organization, we look at culture, systems, procedures, processes, and policies to identify how your business rules constrain or enable resilience, and limit or foster innovation. When considering individuals, we examine their behaviors as well as their attitudes and temperaments to understand their Nimbility.

Use this matrix to quickly identify your business's general level of innovation and resiliency based on your observations.

Why is Nimbility So Important Now?

Amid perpetual upheavals and accelerating world changes, you and your team are amidst transition from the *Experience Economy*, where buyers chose *memorable* outcomes, to the *Transformation Economy*, where buyers choose *meaningful,* authentic, and socially responsible outcomes.

Bringing meaning to customers is now the leading edge of competitive advantage: meaning in being authentically part of community, being environmentally responsible, and being a leader in improving the human condition.

Because your customers want to become a better version of themselves, your company must become a better version of itself.

To do this requires Nimbility.

Navigating Non-stop Upheavals

In today's topsy-turvy, chaotic world, big disasters and big opportunities seem to always be just around the corner. And you've probably noticed that they're occurring faster with more impact than ever before.

Perhaps you see one of these upheavals looming or currently unfolding in your business, and you aren't clear about the best way to utilize it. You are not alone.

The toll of relentless upheavals is more unchecked stress, more disrupted careers, and more uncertainty in business, society, politics, and personal lives. So now, the big question is: how can you align and optimize resources to capitalize on all this chaos instead of being swallowed by it? The answer: become nimble.

Facing Upheavals?

You see these, just as we do. Companies are collapsing under the weight of:

❑ Inflexibility, which prevents nimble navigation of chaos and forced change

❑ Upheaval-skilled leadership deficits – anti-nimbility – which worsen the impact of upheaval

❑ Confusion about how to innovate in a rapidly changing economic, political, and cultural environment, which results in wasted time, energy, mental capacity, and other resources

❑ Uncertainty about how to train executives and teams to surf these changes, instead of being drowned by uncontrollable circumstances.

Our Big Promise

Our promise: to get you to understand what it means to be nimble, to understand the value of Nimbility, and show you a practical path to understanding causes of upheavals and methods to limit their occurrence and impact.

Once you see them, you'll never, ever forget them.

> ONCE YOU EXPERIENCE THE TRUTH, YOU CAN'T UNEXPERIENCE IT.

What This is Not

This book is not a regurgitation of old case studies, old management strategies, and old paradigms. We're not rehashing what no longer works.

Why This Book Is Different

What makes this book different is our approach to developing dynamic, growing businesses in a world of chaos and upheaval through Nimbility. We bring you fresh, new insights along with a synthesis of leading edge, psychologically savvy methods to address your new challenges. It's an optimized and nimble business framework that equips you and your team to become *Upheavals Literate* so you can minimize chaos and capitalize on upheavals.

Written from Deep Knowledge

Dr. David Gruder, PhD (and a lot of other earned honors) is a well published psychologist (writing and contributing to more than 25 books) focusing on business lifecycle psychology, executive performance, culture architecture, and making integrity profitable. He has decades of deep experience in running businesses and nonprofits, and helping other extraordinary leaders resolve seemingly unsolvable business problems. He has delivered speeches, training programs, and consulting in eight countries on three continents.

Mark S.A. Smith is a seasoned business growth strategist with many published books, business guides, and training programs, who works with Fortune 100 companies and startups. With broad international experience, he has delivered more than 2,000 speeches in 54 countries on six continents. He has helped companies bring to market billions of dollars of disruptive technology, researched and developed dozens of business models, sales methods, and marketing strategies. Coaching many executives through business growth and challenging times, he has deep empathy for leadership and broad insight in how to develop and apply systems to deliver consistent results.

We together bring to you a blend of integrated business acumen, deep psychological wisdom, and seasoned systems thinking. And we're always expanding our thought to rapidly adapt to changing world conditions.

A Forward-Looking Perspective on What You Need Now

Academia tends to teach business through case studies that attempt to apply history to the future. This perspective isn't useful amidst rapidly changing business models, changing customer expectations, and market upheavals. You're facing situations that leaders have never seen before, so there aren't many case studies... yet.

> YOU CAN'T NAVIGATE A DYNAMIC MARKET
> THROUGH THE REARVIEW MIRROR.

You won't read a case study or anecdote without our presenting the underlying principles that you can apply to your business and more importantly, the context for when to use the principles or not.

Based on Root-Cause Analysis and Universal Principles

This is a root cause-focused approach to business excellence and success, based on sound psychological principles – understanding your team's way of thinking and aligning leadership – along with sound business principles – involving long-proven ways of structuring and managing business in ways responsive to current circumstances.

It focuses on root cause diagnostics that enable you to discover why an issue is problematic, instead of teaching you symptoms control – attempting short-term management of specific issue instead of resolving them at the root cause level. It offers next generation strategic and tactical frameworks that build in psychological savvy each step of the way, so you don't fall into the trap of short-term, unsustainable inspirational/motivational/wishful thinking.

Embraces the Required Diversity to Succeed

We discuss what's required for the diverse perspectives and strengths to come together to successfully communicate, collaborate, and innovate, routinely and consistently, without necessarily having to schedule specific innovation or brainstorming events, which often feel good but far too rarely produce tangible results.

How to Get the Most Out of This Book

Because of ongoing, nonstop business disruptions, you might be feeling burnt out, tired, or discouraged. Hang in there. We wrote this book to bring you a fresh, new, revitalizing vision that sparks authentic hope for your future.

We suggest that you first skim this book to identify relevant topics. You'll notice there aren't dense blocks of text because executives learn in short chunks. Scan through, read the headings and memes, and only stop and dig in where we spark your attention.

Then, as a colleague suggests, "Go through it in first gear." Take time to digest, debate, question, consider, adapt, and ultimately guide your team to a new vision. If you need to discuss some of these points, contact us, and one of us, or one of our team members, will be glad to help. Learn more on page 199.

Here are a few ways to get the most from your investment in reading this.

Get Ready to Unlearn and Learn

Are you willing to unlearn and relearn? This book requires you to suspend judgement so you can see the big picture we are painting, decide which specifics will be right for you, and then bring them to your team.

> THE ILLITERATE OF THE 21ST CENTURY WILL NOT BE
> THOSE WHO CANNOT READ AND WRITE,
> BUT THOSE WHO CANNOT LEARN, UNLEARN, AND RELEARN.
> – ALVIN TOFFLER

A potential blind spot for you is believing your current organizational design and business model is what will continue to work for you. We call resistance to required change *Paradigm Attachment Disorder* – the insistence that your experience, the box you're in right now that's been created by your identity and culture, will always work in the future. With the radical changes in the business world, paradigm attachment destroys the Nimbility that is required to navigate upheavals and massive changes.

Use this book to help you unlearn and learn. Underline phrases, circle paragraphs, fold down pages, make notes, note your points of opposite opinion. A pristine book doesn't work as well as one that's marked up and mutilated. Don't worry, you can get another copy for your archives.

The bad news: most of what you and your team know won't work in the future.

> "IN TIMES OF CHANGE,
> LEARNERS INHERIT THE EARTH,
> WHILE THE LEARNED FIND THEMSELVES
> BEAUTIFULLY EQUIPPED TO DEAL WITH A WORLD
> THAT NO LONGER EXISTS."
> – ERIC HOFFER

The good news: your cognitive capacity, your ability to handle complexity and figure it out from the proper perspective, will be your most valuable asset.

We are going to push you out of your comfort zone. Will you be okay with us challenging you? Are you ready to handle whatever truths you discover as you apply the principles and perspectives we provide?

If not, save yourself some grief and put this book down.

If so, let's go!

Boldly Go Where You Haven't Been

Nimbility is being able to conceive of a future that doesn't yet exist, that you'll create using methods you haven't yet experienced nor invented.

This requires courage to focus on the strategic and objective *what* that you're going to do, and the motivational *why* that you're doing it, without yet knowing the tactical *how* that you'll get it done.

Can you allow this new vision to emerge in the face of doubt and uncertainty of how you'll get it done?

> "STORM YOUR OWN GATES OR OTHERS WILL."
> – CHRIS STARK

What to Expect

The future is a moving target and Nimbility is about surfing the chaos to create a business that is sustainable, scalable, profitable, and ultimately, saleable.

Some of what you'll read you already know. We'll be challenging you to think about it in a new way.

Some of the things you'll discover, you used to do. We'll remind you that it's time to do them again.

And, without a doubt, we have many new ideas for you. When you choose to use them, you'll become as successful as you wish.

Are you ready for the transformation?

A Final Note on Our Writing Style

You may notice some intentional minor repetition as you read. This is because we want skimming readers to get the idea in context without having to read this book from beginning to end. We've also included a few key ideas from the companion book, *The Nimble C-Suite* to ensure full understanding of key concepts.

When we use *or* in a list of options, assume that it's an *inclusive or*, meaning the list could be *and, or*, or *all* items listed. This keeps us from using the clumsy *and/or* reference. If it's any different, we'll be explicit in our writing.

Chapter Summary

❑ Disruptive forces rock traditional business models and threaten your livelihood.

❑ Responding well to these disruptions counterintuitively requires you to change leadership and business models, embracing Nimbility to go from surviving to thriving.

❑ Changing leadership models requires your willingness as a business executive to become nimble and explore strategies and tactics that haven't been used before.

Ask Yourself

- ❏ What have I noticed about the disruptions my business is facing and the changes my business is faced with making?
- ❏ How is our lack of Nimbility impacting our present and future?
- ❏ How could becoming Nimble create a better path to future success?
- ❏ Am I willing to invest time and energy to uplevel my leadership so we can exploit the new business realities?

Ask Your Team

- ❏ What changes do we need to make to be more relevant to our customers and become more valuable to our target market?
- ❏ What would it be worth for us to do that?
- ❏ What would it cost if we didn't do that?

Action Plan

- ❏ Keep reading.
- ❏ Mark up this book, take notes, bend over pages.
- ❏ Determine who else needs to read this. Buy them a copy and have them debate the concepts with you and each other.

Chapter 2:
What Allows Upheavals?

A nimble executive knows what allows upheavals, and so can spot them and harness them for the betterment of the company. In this chapter we explore factors that allow upheavals and limit Nimbility.

Let's start with the three that we see have the next biggest impact, following after the C-Suite issues discussed in the prior chapter.

There are three fundamental conditions that allow upheavals in a world of well-meaning leaders: *blind spots*, *misunderstandings*, and *withholds*. Until a team is upheavals literate, identifying and eliminating all three of these requires external intervention, because if you could spot these yourself, you wouldn't find yourself or your company engulfed by upheavals.

Blind Spots

Blind spots are issues, attitudes, and skill deficits that you are unaware of. You don't know what you don't know. Arrogant, narcissistic, and self-important leadership creates massive blind spots because these people declare that they don't have them.

> ORGANIZATIONAL CULTURES TEND TO INADVERTENTLY PROMOTE
> BLIND SPOTS THAT CAUSE THEIR BUSINESS TO ULTIMATELY FAIL.
> INNOVATION STARTS WITH ELIMINATING THOSE BLIND SPOTS.

The first step to blind spotting is to admit you have blind spots and open yourself to others pointing them out to you.

The concept of a blind spot comes from the physical fact that human eyes have a blind spot where the optic nerve connects to the eyeball. You can't see these unless you actively look for them.

Want to observe your blind spot? Hold this page about a page width from your face. Focus on the **X** below and close your right eye. Move the book slowly towards and away from you and the **O** will disappear and reappear from view.

O   X

You can do this with your right eye by focusing on the **O**, closing your left eye, and watch the **X** disappear and reappear.

Notice that there isn't a hole in your vision. Your brain fills in the gap with an image that is like the surrounding area; in other words, with false information.

Have you ever played the card game, Solitaire? If so, you may have noticed that an observer watching you play can spot moves you can't immediately see. You've probably been in both roles, as the player and the observer. Have you ever felt smug as an observer offering advice and annoyed as a player receiving it?

You might have these same reactions when you first notice a blind spot or one of yours is pointed out to you. These are not resourceful responses. Instead, point out blind spots with empathy because we all have them, and receive blind spotting with gratitude, as they are doing you a favor, even if you initially feel annoyed.

You may have realized that your most consistent personal blind spotter is your significant other. That realization probably made you laugh.

Many an upheaval has manifested because blind spots have ultimately blindsided the leader and their organization. This can include corporate culture blind spots where taboo topics mask impending upheavals.

THE BIGGEST EXECUTIVE BLIND SPOT:
THINKING ABOUT YOUR FUTURE
FROM THE CONTEXT OF THE PAST.

Blind spots also get activated when unexpected or foreseen internal or external forces are downplayed or entirely ignored.

Create a Blindspotting Culture

In gymnastics and at the gym when lifting, you have a spotter whose responsibility is your safety. They are there so you can attempt new moves or lift heavier weights that are outside your comfort zone. They make your expansion safe.

This same principle applies to your team's trouble-shooting, innovation, and exploration. A way that everyone can have each other's back is to blindspot ideas so everyone remains safe.

In nimble cultures, everyone on your team is a spotter who shares responsibility for safety. This stability helps make it safe to create outside the lines. It's safe to leave your comfort zone because you have spotters that keep you safe.

What Being a Spotter Is and Isn't

A spotter doesn't gossip, snitch, tattle, shame, blame, manipulate, be arrogant or judgmental, seek revenge, carry out vendettas, or act like a victim. They aren't a self-appointed savior or enforcement agent. And they aren't someone who breaks confidentiality by divulging private information publicly or by telling others something that was said to them in confidence.

Rather, a spotter is someone who cares deeply about an organization's success, about developing or maintaining a healthy company culture, and about elevating brand integrity. When a spotter detects a possible blind-spot that could be harmful to success, culture, or brand, they offer that information to someone who will be able to make wiser decisions with that information than without it.

How to Be a Spotter

Here are five steps in being a truly helpful spotter:

❑ Remember that everyone in a company is a spotter because part of being human is to have blind spots, and that a sign of maturity to be receptive to the illumination of potential blind spots.

❑ Commit to being a blindspotter who abstains from doing this in harmful ways like those listed at the start of this section. In other words, make sure your motives are authentically noble.

❑ Before bringing a potential blindspot to someone's attention, make sure you select the right person to bring it to (someone who will be able to make wiser decisions with that information than without it), and that you're in a heartset of love.[3]

❑ Inform your chosen person about the potential blindspot in private and without shame or blame. Also let them know your deepest concerns about the harm this blind spot might cause and your highest intentions about the positive things that could come from illuminating this blind spot, so they are fully clear about the noble reasons you're bringing this to them.

❑ Let go of attachment to outcomes. A spotter's role is to offer information that might be unrecognized, not to be in charge of decisions that are made as a result of providing that information.

Spotter Team Training

Becoming a truly helpful spotter requires not only the willingness to do blindspotting on behalf of an organization's wellbeing, but the willingness of the organization and all of its leaders to be blindspotted. Establishing this

---

[3] When we refer to love, we mean *Agape*, a Greco-Christian term referring to unconditional love, the highest form of love and charity, and the love between a Higher Power and humanity.

willingness and becoming adept at truly helpful blind-spotting often requires training, since most people have never been taught how to do this in good ways. As adept blindspotters and blindspotting trainers, we stand ready to help.

Misunderstandings

Misunderstandings happen when what a leader thinks is true, isn't. This often occurs when a leader or their team cling to an understanding that is *True But Not Useful, True But Incomplete,* or *Was True But Isn't Now.*

Often these misunderstandings are the second- and third-order effects of prior decisions, where a leader blindly insists on continuing to stand behind their decisions because they don't fully grasp their unintended negative consequences, which we call *impact literacy deficits.*

Solving this requires constant questioning of situations and contexts, comparing what is held to be true against unchanging leadership and business principles, and frequently reviewing tactical methods that must constantly change in response to shifting conditions.

Misunderstandings also ensue when a leader mistakenly views a tactic as a strategy. This most often occurs in leaders who rapidly ascend from tactical implementation roles without formal top-flight strategic leadership training.

Withholds

Withholds happen when someone with critical information doesn't share it because they believe it's politically unsound to do so, or they judge it as less important than it really is because they don't understand the priorities, or they are attempting a power play.

Withholds can be prevented by installing blameless communication methods into your culture, through your willingness as a leader to continuously train your team on priorities, and through taking the time to seek and sincerely consider multiple perspectives before deciding what to do. We recommend using the Upgraded Whistleblower strategy outlined following.

Withholds can be inadvertently invited. For example, if you ask for *advice* and frequently choose to take a different approach than the advice offered, the advice giver may conclude that you don't value their advice and stop offering it. The solution is to *stop* asking for advice and instead ask for *perspective*.

Reflect on this approach: "As I consider our options, I value your perspective. I'll be asking others for their perspective, too, before making a decision. Tell me your thoughts about..."

Eliminate Withholds Through the Upleveled Whistleblower

A powerful way to eliminate withholds is through the upleveled whistleblower. In the traditional context, whistleblowers exposed malfeasance or fraud, potentially subjecting them to repercussions and attack.

In nimble organizations, whistleblowers become valued blindspotters who bring important information to strategic and tactical decision-makers that might otherwise remain hidden, buried, or ignored by management. We reframe the whistleblower as a blindspotter.

Who might be a blindspotter in nimble organizations? Anyone! This is because in nimble organizations, transparency is the antidote to unforeseen upheavals, and freely sharing information is part of the culture. Let's now expand on this to map an escalation path that shows blindspotters how to best route their information.

Establish a Clear Escalation Path

The right escalation path means that potentially critical information efficiently travels up the command structure without friction, blame, or shame, which keeps vital intelligence flowing to prevent, detect, or address potential upheavals. See Figure 2.

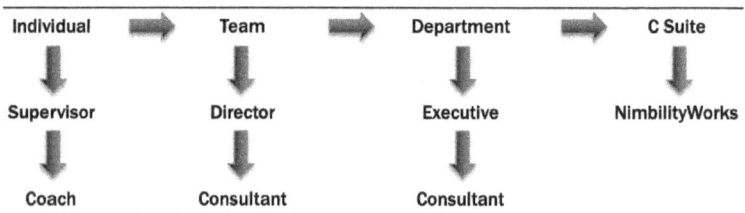

Individual ➡	Team ➡	Department ➡	C Suite
⬇	⬇	⬇	⬇
Supervisor	Director	Executive	NimbilityWorks
⬇	⬇	⬇	
Coach	Consultant	Consultant	

Figure 2: Define an Escalation Path for Information Flow and Access to Additional Skills

The individual who is part of a department team can question their supervisor. If the supervisor needs more skills, they can access a coach (either internal or external) for further development.

The supervisor can question their director. If the director needs more skills, they can access a consultant (either internal or external).

The director can question the executive – either vice president or chief officer. If the executive needs more skills, they can access a consultant (either internal or external).

The chief officer can question their peers or access an executive consultant or mentor.[4]

Inability to Conduct Respectful Debate

A key contributor to the three deficits discussed above is the inability to conduct respectful debate. Many, if not most, people seem to have lost the skill of respectfully debating ideas. When engaging in a conflicting conversation, these too often rapidly deteriorate into personal attacks or withdrawal. This allows upheavals.

> WHAT WE CAN'T DISCUSS, WE CAN'T SOLVE.

Some possible causes for this:
- ❏ A corporate culture that avoids conflict and debate
- ❏ Poorly modeled conflict management on TV and in movies, often ending in revenge not resolution
- ❏ TV "news" programming featuring arguing, overtalking, lack of respect, either-or extremes in positions, and belittling of opposite viewpoints, all of which models dysfunctional debate instead of illuminating the virtues of multiple perspectives. (Bruce Raymond Wright's book, *The Apples of Your Genius*, offers valuable upgrades to your capacity to weigh multiple perspectives.)

---

[4] We at the NimbilityWorks are here to help. Let's talk. See more on page 199.

❑ Unrestrained and consequence-free personal attacks on social media for one's beliefs, opinions, and positions

❑ Avoidance of conflict because of the fear of rejection and perceived potential career impact

❑ Lack of true debate training in school, where one must effectively argue both sides of a position

❑ Poorly modeled conflicting conversations by family and friends, ending in stonewalling, the silent treatment, shaming, and shunning

❑ A school system that rewards rote recall and discourages discovery, discussion, creativity, innovation, and true collaboration

❑ A personal identity with a high need to be right (paradigm attachment disorder) versus needing to understand multiple perspectives

❑ Viewpoints set by leadership that cannot be questioned or challenged

❑ Peer groups, including executive and tactical teams, that engage in groupthink and reject outside ideas.

Repairing this societal dysfunctionality in business requires new skills for communication, discussion, debate, conflict management, and collaboration, along with a culture that embraces debate and exploring diverse ideas.

How is your team's lack of discussion and debate skills impacting your organization? What upheavals will this gap attract?

Insisting on Stability at All Costs

Let's now consider other factors that allow upheavals and restrict Nimbility. Traditional factories were designed and built over years to deliver goods that would be in the market for decades. Those market slots are full and being disrupted at every turn.

We're seeing well-run companies stumbling because they can't move fast enough to keep up with the demands of their nimble – and fickle – customers. Think about how Dollar Shave Club wounded Gillette so much that they are, as we write this, scrambling to catch up.

Traditional business models create a static system with so much inertia that meaningful change becomes a challenge; they are anti-nimble. People involved don't want to change, management sees change as risky to their career, and change creates costs and inefficiencies counter to their business model. And they have plenty of evidence that seems to support their position, called *confirmation bias* where one cherry picks the data to support their belief.

Yet, in today's rapidly moving world, the merely efficient get left behind. Businesses are closing at an unprecedented rate (largely because of debt overload) despite previous all-time record highs on Wall Street. If you're stuck in your processes, you're at risk of being disrupted, and you won't detect it until it's too late.

> "THAT'S HOW WE'VE ALWAYS DONE IT" INDICATES A FEAR OF FACING THE TRUTH, AND THIS IN TURN INVITES WITHHOLDS.

What has to change?

The Transformation to Nimbility

Choosing a business model that embraces ever-changing technology and market demands requires corporate-wide flexibility and a willingness to forgo false certainty for true uncertainty. Even massive companies must be able to pivot in months if not weeks. For example, the day of an 18-month I.T. project is coming to an end. It's been replaced with rapid phased, scalable deployments in the cloud: think lean and agile management methods on steroids.

Lack of Execution Risk Management

The biggest issue with moving from efficiency to flexibility is execution risk: how can your team execute when they don't know what they'll be doing? This requires a new executive mindset, new tools, new reward structures, a new business model, and specific people in place with unique attitudes and skills that might never before have been needed. We discuss execution risk factors in detail starting on page 37.

Culture Shift

And it takes more than those changes. It also takes a massive culture shift. See Figure 3.

The Nimble C-Suite

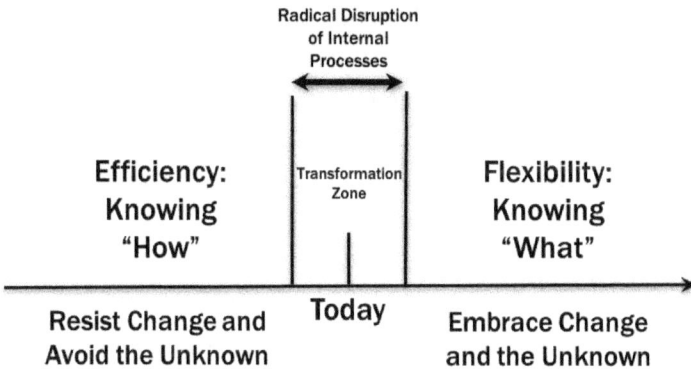

Radical Disruption
of Internal
Processes

⬅➡

| Efficiency: Knowing "How" | Transformation Zone | Flexibility: Knowing "What" |

Resist Change and   **Today**   Embrace Change
Avoid the Unknown   and the Unknown

Figure 3: The Transformation from Efficiency to Flexibility

Making the transformation from using efficiency as a key value to using flexibility as a key value demands massive cultural disruption of internal processes, politics, and procedures. It's not for the faint of heart or the indecisive. Entering the transformation zone requires a complete overhaul of what's judged as right and wrong, what's judged as good business and bad business. It requires a complete reinvention of the organization and culture from the ground up.

At least one third of the existing companies won't make this transition, can't make this transition, and will make every excuse on the planet to avoid this transformation. Mark our words: we'll see those companies on the scrap heap, in the bargain bin, and in MBA case studies of failures.

Efficiency requires expert understanding of the tactical *how* to accomplish a task or mission. The better you know how, the more efficient you become. Much corporate resistance to change stems from a tendency to avoid the unknown because of fear of upsetting existing processes and fear of the chaos that can result. Better to master the art of surfing upset and chaos so flourishing results.

> "HOW CAN I MANAGE CHAOS?"
> "YOU DON'T. YOU SURF CHAOS."

Becoming agile and flexible changes the focus to a strategic *what* that has to be accomplished, and knowing that the tactical *how* is always a moving target. The faster you can identify the *what*, the sooner you'll be able to figure out – or outsource – the *how*. To do this, you and your team must embrace the unknown, viewing every day as an adventure and an opportunity to be seized.

> KNOWING HOW TO ACHIEVE YOUR VISION
> ALWAYS FOLLOWS CLARITY OF YOUR VISION.
> NEVER THE OTHER WAY AROUND.

Transformation Deficits

Without the ability to navigate transformation, you'll be allowing upheavals. How can you transition to agility, flexibility, and Nimbility? Consider these ideas.

Create a Culture of Speed

Stop the culture of "we need more data" and "let's decide next quarter." Instead, bring together the brightest new minds and put them into regular scrums so you can "skate to where the puck's gonna be," to use a Wayne

Gretsky metaphor. Take on the mindset of an entrepreneurial startup, willing and able to pivot as you get more intelligence.

Embrace Agile and Lean Methods

These methods allow rapidly adjusting processes, and quickly correcting issues, so products can take flight fast. There are lots of great books on this topic, many excellent facilitators, and experienced team members who are ready to take your processes and products to a new level.

Expect Massive Fallout

In our experience, when you make massive transformation, one third of your team won't make it. It's too much for them to handle. The sooner you move them on, the smoother the transformation will be. If you don't, their fear and blindness will actively sabotage the transition and thoughtlessly take down your company. You probably know who they are. While these are good people who provided valuable service in the past, they are unable make the journey to the new world. Instead of letting them tank your business, let them go for the good of everyone else.

> CUT LOOSE THE CHRONIC NAYSAYERS TODAY.

One third will be on the fence. The sooner you can win them over, the better off you'll be. Without a solid plan and swift execution, you risk losing half of them, and this might terminate your transition.

And one third will be on board from the start. "It's about time! I thought I'd have to leave." These are your transformation champions. Round them up, give them the new direction, and get out of their way.

Turn the Young Generation Loose on the Problem

The good news: Millennials and Gen-Z already know how to make rapid transformation based on their extensive experience playing video games. They live to level up. In that environment, they're not afraid to make mistakes because they know they'll learn fast and will quickly take another shot with another approach.

While Boomers and some Gen Xs may resist this idea, the young generation excels and will, by default, soon be running the world. If this freaks you out, you're in for a massive surprise because you're resisting the inevitable.

Get Help

Get help from those who have previously paid the "stupid tax" on transformations like this. They know how. We at NimbilityWorks can help. Learn more on page 199.

Chapter Summary

❑ Common company deficits actually allow and invite upheavals. These must be first addressed for a company to become nimble.

❑ There are three main enablers of upheavals: blind spots, misunderstandings, and withholds.

❑ To eliminate these upheavals enablers, you must install a blindspotting culture, which encourages calling out issues that can result in an upheaval.

❑ To eliminate withholds, define a clear escalation path so that your team can provide critical insight without fear of negative career impact.

❑ The inability to conduct respectful debate severely limits Nimbility. Foster the required skills, guidelines, and permission for any member of your team to be able to initiate a potentially contentious discussion.

❑ Demanding stability limits innovation and resilience, and so destroys Nimbility.

❑ Lack of execution risk management allows upheavals – seen and unforeseen – to manifest.

❑ Limits to the company's ability to transform has substantial impact on Nimbility.

Ask Yourself

❑ How do I handle blind spotting? Do I embrace or resist the insight?

❑ What has been the impact of misunderstandings on my company? Do I still cling to old decisions or positions that no longer serve me?

❑ Have I fostered a culture of withholding? If so, what's been the impact on our Nimbility?

❑ Does my team have a clear, blameless escalation path to alert me and my team to impending problems?

❑ How do we handle conflict and debate? Do I have a deficit that's limiting innovation and resilience?

❑ What's my attitude on stability: do I insist upon it or can I effectively balance stability with change?

❑ How aware am I about execution risk? Do I really understand the factors to correctly direct the team for resilient operations?

❑ What's my track record on leading transformation? Where are my gaps? What will I do about upleveling this skill?

Ask Your Team

- ❏ What blind spots are we ignoring at our peril?
- ❏ How comfortable are you at pointing out another's blind spot?
- ❏ How comfortable are you with someone telling you about a blind spot?
- ❏ Where could we be making assumptions that lead to misunderstandings?
- ❏ Have you ever kept information from a manager or executive because you were afraid of the potential damage to your career? What impact did you observe from this choice?
- ❏ Do you think we have a blameless escalation path for when information should be shared up the command chain?
- ❏ How well do we as a company handle conflict and debate? If we could improve these skills, what do you think would be the outcome?
- ❏ From your perspective, do we focus too much on stability or change? What's the impact of this focus?
- ❏ Do you feel that you have a good handle on the execution risk factors we need to consider in this business climate, or do we need to conduct a formal review to make sure we understand all of the potential issues?
- ❏ How well do you think we handle transformation, where we need to make sweeping changes to stay current and relevant to our customers?

Action Plan

- ❏ Identify the active factors that allow upheavals in your company.

❑ Prioritize the top three to address immediately.
❑ Create a plan for culture adjustment, training, and coaching to permanently fix these problems.
❑ Get help if necessary, to clarify the path and process.

Chapter 3:
Sources and Root Causes of Upheavals

In this chapter, we'll discuss the sources of upheaval and their root causes. These manifest as execution risk factors which, when unaddressed, can at worst trigger massive chaos and business failure. At the least these will distract your team from innovation and consume critical resources that should be devoted to remaining resilient and competitive.

New Market and Business Forces Drive Upheavals

New market and business forces that were ignored or downplayed now have much greater impact. If your team is blind to these factors, you're at high risk of upheaval.

Technology Capability Acceleration

Technology changes exponentially (doubling in capability and value every 12 to 24 months, observed by Moore's[5] Law and Metcalfe's Law[6]) while organizations

---

[5] en.wikipedia.org/wiki/Moore%27s_law
[6] en.wikipedia.org/wiki/Metcalfe%27s_law

tend to change logarithmically (compound increases of annual growth with the rate declining over time).

Scott Brinker dubbed this observation Martec's Law in 2013.[7] See Figure 4.[8]

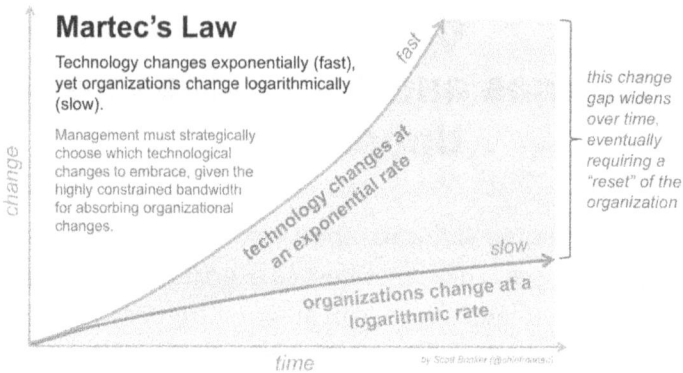

Martec's Law

Technology changes exponentially (fast), yet organizations change logarithmically (slow).

Management must strategically choose which technological changes to embrace, given the highly constrained bandwidth for absorbing organizational changes.

this change gap widens over time, eventually requiring a "reset" of the organization

technology changes at an exponential rate

organizations change at a logarithmic rate

time

Figure 4: Martec's Law Describes Organizational Resets Driven by Technology

Brinker noted that management must strategically choose which changes to deploy because traditional business organizations get overwhelmed by too much change. Of course, this was prior to the concept of Nimbility.

In time, the gap widens until the organization is forced into a drastic reset, gets acquired, or closes. Technological change rapidly outstrips an organization's ability to change unless they actively and culturally embrace technology advances. Martec's Law explains why once-

[7] chiefmartec.com/2013/06/martecs-law-technology-changes-exponentially-organizations-change-logarithmically/
[8] Graphic used with kind permission from Scott Brinker.

solid companies can rapidly disappear, such as Kodak ignoring digital photography and Blockbuster ignoring Internet movie streaming.

> AS TECHNOLOGY ACCELERATES,
> THE FUTURE BELONGS TO THOSE
> WHO CAN UNLEARN FASTEST.

We are in a time of extreme technology change, with rapidly increasing compute power, storage capacity, and network bandwidth. This change accelerates in every subsequent generation of technology development.

For example, expect accelerating market upheavals as the next generation of cellular technology brings substantially faster bandwidth to your handheld device, disrupting customer experience expectations (instant access), media consumption habits (abandonment of cable TV), ubiquitous data collection (everyone holds a measuring device plus the Internet of Things everywhere), wearable technology (augmented reality glasses and implants, also called the Internet of Bodies, IoB) and perhaps new illnesses from some of these technologies that have been inadequately safety-tested.

Unless you actively and culturally embrace technology advances and are on the lookout for potential unintended negative consequences of these, you will be left behind as tech savvy companies embrace technology faster than you do, or go down in flames because they ignored safety or ethics issues. It's highly likely that your tactical, Chief Information Officer is holding you back.

We discuss why this is often the case in detail in the companion book, *The Nimble C-Suite.*

Disruptive Generational Shifts

Generations are defined by key political, economic, and social factors that impact identity and life goals.[9]

While the Boomer generation (born 1946 – 1964) is retiring from the C-Suite, there are many still running boards of directors, using that generation's world view in their governance. They direct Gen X (born 1965 – 1980) and Millennials (born 1981 – 1996) who are selling to Gen Z (born 1997 – 2012) with Gen Alpha (born after 2012) following.

While, at this writing, Gen Alpha is very young, they are predicted to be the most transformative generation so far, with their key worldview influences being driven by COVID lockdowns, remote learning experiences, social justice initiatives, and a life of continuous upheavals. They and Gen Z have great influence on their parents' purchasing decisions, insisting on buying from socially responsible companies and choosing Earth-friendly lifestyles, such as veganism. They reject traditional capitalism (actually, they reject sociopathic capitalism) and lean towards socialistic thinking, often because they have not been exposed to frameworks for socially responsible capitalism.

---

[9] These are the Pew Research definitions of generations. www.pewresearch.org/fact-tank/2019/01/17/where-millennials-end-and-generation-z-begins/

For example, many major US food producers claim to use only cage-free eggs.[10] In a traditional, cost-driven business model, this would be unthinkable. Why would you pay substantially more for a commodity that is formulaically indistinguishable from its much less expensive alternative? That's the power of generational insistence on social responsibility.

How prepared for this are you and your executive team?

The New Impact of Autism

Increasing autism in these generations – some experts shockingly predict one out of two in this decade – alters the makeup of the workforce and customer base. *Neurodiversity* (a newer term for those with autistic characteristics, ADHD, and so forth) changes requirements for hiring, behavior management, and skills development.

Neurodiversity has the potential to expand team effectiveness; however, this also requires new approaches to roles, workplace environment, management methods, and personnel development plans. Neurodiverse customers also have unique requirements that will most likely change how you approach product development, marketing, sales, product packaging, delivery, and customer service. Both of us are on the neurodiverse spectrum, embracing the gifts it brings.

---

[10] blog.humanesociety.org/2021/01/major-corporations-including-nestle-and-arbys-confirm-they-now-use-100-cage-free-eggs-in-u-s.html

Neurotypical customers (for instance, those not on the autism and ADHD spectrums) who have strong social awareness tend to avoid companies that aren't adaptive to neurodiverse customers because those folks are among their friends and family members.

Are you preparing and training your team to successfully service a fuller range of neurodiversity?

Common Sources and Causes of Upheavals

We've cataloged sources of upheavals that we've observed over our many decades of working with executives and their teams. While this list is long and comprehensive, it's by no means complete.

We fully expect that you have addressed many of these risk issues. Yet we also want to make sure you don't have any blind spots about this. As you review the list, identify your own additional sources of execution risk and actively address them.

Risks are organized into two main categories: *internal* causes of upheaval and *external* causes of upheaval. These categories are subdivided into four varieties: *preventable, unnecessary, foreseeable,* and *surprise.*

The Pending Upheavals Assessment

Let's assess your execution risk factors. As you read this chapter, assess for your company which factors are: (1) not present, (2) visible but not a current threat, (3) possible but invisible, (4) visible and threatening, and (5) a current impact factor.

The *Pending Upheaval Score* this generates gives you an accurate read on your current level of execution risk and clarity about where you need to focus attention right now. The higher the score, the higher your risk.

Culture-Driven Upheavals

We start with culture because it has the greatest impact on your executive team, your execution team, your customers, and ultimately, your brand experience.

Culture defines how you treat each other and ultimately how you treat your customer. It's what you stand for and what you won't stand for. Culture defines the identity of your company and overrides any other declarations or business rules.

> CULTURE EATS STRATEGY FOR BREAKFAST. – PETER DRUCKER

Culture decides who you hire and who you don't, how you interact, who you'll do business with, who will be your vendors, and how you develop your team.

If you don't have a defined and reinforced culture, it will default to the lowest cultural denominator in which the bar is set by your company's lowest performers, because that's what's tolerated.

Your Culture Manifesto Sets the Scene

One of the best culture documents was created decades ago by Mark DiMassimo, founder of DigoBrands.com, a NY-based marketing agency with a roster of household-name clients. This thoughtful and comprehensive culture definition has led them to become a top agency that is highly sought after by companies that inspire change.

Mark publicly offers his culture document for your inspiration.[11]

Disclosure: Mark is a co-founder of NimbilityWorks, along with us. Even if he wasn't, we'd still recommend his culture manifesto because it's that good.

Review your culture statements against the upheaval sources in this chapter so you can more effectively limit your exposure to execution risk and increase your Nimbility.

Internal Foreseeable Culture-Driven Upheavals

"Don't-Discuss" Topic Boundaries

If your undefined culture demands that certain topics are not discussed, these *don't talk* rules create culture-induced blind spots. This can happen when an executive dismisses a topic, belittles a topic, or says "I won't talk about that."

Undefined Responsibility and Accountability

When government passes legislation but doesn't fund it, it's dead. Likewise, when a strategic initiative is launched without an accountable executive and responsible execution leader, it's dead.

Often this happens when an executive makes a decision and assigns execution ad hoc to someone who may not have the mindset, skillset, time, or budget resources to execute. This in turn tends to overwhelm the team, depress their performance, and impacts other important business functions.

---

[11] Get the DiGo culture manifesto at digobrands.com/digo-brands-a-culture

{ 44 }

Chain of Command Communication Blocks

While chain of command is important to keeping information flow in the right channels of accountability and responsibly, it can also stifle critical information flow. The management chain must be willing to hear information and determine root cause issues without fear of upstream and downstream career impact.

As one of our mentors taught, "I don't like surprises. Bring me your challenges along with your proposed solution as soon as you can, because I have access to resources and perspective that you might not have, which we can use to solve the problem sooner rather than later."

> YOU CAN USE AN ERASER ON THE DRAFTING TABLE
> OR A SLEDGEHAMMER ON THE CONSTRUCTION SITE.
> – FRANK LLOYD WRIGHT

An engineering axiom is that fixing a problem gets at least ten times more expensive each time it increments through the design, production, and customer delivery process. If a flaw slips past an early stage and gets to the customer, it becomes extremely expensive to deal with, as we've seen with the Boeing 737 Max and the NASA Challenger disaster.

With an open communication channel, information that prevents upheavals can easily flow to the level where it can be addressed, and disaster prevented. We discuss how to do this on page 24.

Impact Literacy

Impact literacy is the skill of being able to foresee primary, secondary, and tertiary effects of a decision, and to repair and learn from any effects that are not seen beforehand.

Low levels of impact literacy in your company means you have people who cannot foresee the impacts of their actions beyond their own positive or negative experience. Like a child gleefully running to pet a wild animal without thought of how that animal may respond to its perceived threat, low impact literacy regularly triggers unexpected upheavals and disasters when impulsive employees exceed a boundary. These are preventable upheavals. Corporate politics based in low impact literacy causes massive amounts of unnecessary upheaval.

When your personnel have high impact literacy, they think beyond only their own benefits, to the benefits of all those involved.

Impact literacy becomes even more vital when you are a ESG or TBL company; everyone must understand their impact on social issues, planet, and profit, not only their team or themselves.[12]

Human Resources Misalignment of Policing and Quality Control

While it's common for HR to implement policy policing and deal with performance issues, this approach to HR limits its ability to fulfill its intended function, which is to uplevel human talent.

---

[12] ESG (Environmental, Social, Governance) and TBL (Triple Bottom Line) are guiding principles for socially responsible companies, which we discuss in depth in the companion book, *The Nimble C-Suite*.

HR too often ends up dealing out punitive measures instead of elevating the mindsets and skills necessary for talent development. If HR is involved in training, it's most often check-the-box-for-a-government-mandate training. These include training such as sexual harassment, drug usage, and theft, and these behavioral norms should be clearly spelled out in your culture manifesto.

When companies focus only on these HR dimensions, they are trying to control symptoms instead of resolving underlying causes. Instead of resolving issues, this approach fuels behavior problems that don't go away.

HR's function has too frequently devolved into a recruiting stop for discussing policy and benefits, and being a gatekeeper for keeping poor talent under control instead of helping them develop.

Our solution is to split HR into three separate departments: talent recruitment & development, policy enforcement, and benefits administration. That's because these functions are not compatible with each other; it's not possible for one person or department to excel at wearing all of these hats at the same time.

Talent recruitment & development gets moved to the Chief Integrity Officer, as described in depth in the companion book, *The Nimble C-Suite*, in which we also discuss the upleveled Chief Personnel Development Officer replacing HR. This is a T-Suite (Tactical Suite) role.

Learned Helplessness

Impact illiteracy is an outgrowth of, and reinforced by, learned helplessness. That's a psychological term for a belief that one's choices don't affect others. Doing something positive doesn't make a difference. Doing something negative doesn't make a difference. Learned helplessness lives at the heart of victim thinking.

You've probably noticed that some people are becoming less and less capable of figuring things out for themselves. If they haven't been trained, they refuse to do a task. When they face a new challenge, they lock up and can't make progress. When challenged, they melt down into a messy puddle. They refuse to take responsibility and accountability; they whine that everything is always someone or something else's fault, operating in perpetual victim mode.

All of these symptoms are indications of learned helplessness, a growing behavioral problem that is reinforced by inept schooling systems that reward participation instead of excellence, that cave into parental indulgence, and that thwart critical skills development. Mediocre behavior by students at the institutional level, and mediocre educational policies at the governance level, have been overly tolerated for far too long. Among many other things, this has led to mediocre teachers being retained and talented teachers being hamstrung.

Are your employee's parents calling to defend their child's unacceptable behaviors and demand certain outcomes? Not directly, but their ghosts are continuing to influence your personnel's attitudes.

Some people in the workforce are essentially children in adult bodies who are without adult skills. They have no shame, no social skills, no impact literacy, and no self-responsibility. They often live in their parent's basement and, for them, work becomes a play date, not a serious endeavor. Are we being too harsh? Perhaps, although we are simply reporting here a common problem we hear about from our clients.

Tolerating learned helplessness in your company invites upheavals. Plus, learned helplessness is virtually impossible to resolve in a crisis. It is therefore crucial that you assess talent for learned helplessness levels, and that you implement ongoing comprehensive training in self-responsibility and impact-literate decision-making skills that enable people to recover from learned helplessness. Employees who don't embody the skills they're taught in these programs must be released or they become an unaddressed source of upheavals and lawsuits.

Missing Accountability Procedure for Commitment

Effective accountability requires commitment. This requires creating *accountability-capable agreements*. We discuss this in depth on page 169.

What too often passes for a commitment is a good intention. A good intention sounds like this: "Let's get together for lunch." An accountability-capable agreement sounds like this: "So, we've agreed to get together for lunch at Joe's Luncheonette on March 12 at 12:30 pm, and that if either of us is going to be delayed we will immediately notify the other."

A good intention is vague, so it's impossible to tell whether it's been done. Accountability is specific and includes an updates agreement.

For example, in a family meeting about chores, your teenager says, "I'll take out the garbage." (We know, them just saying that might feel like a miracle!)

That's merely a good intention. Think about it: what's missing? Now, think about your teen saying, "I will empty all the wastebaskets in our house, except for the ones in everyone's bedroom except my own, no later than 7:00 pm every Tuesday night. I will then take the trash and recycling bins to the curb no later than 7:15pm every Tuesday night. I will retrieve them on Wednesday when I get home from school or by noon when school is out."

Do you now see the difference between a good intention and an accountability-capable agreement?

Confusing good intentions with commitments is the cause of untold numbers of avoidable conflicts at work and at home. Only an accountability-capable agreement is a commitment. Everything else is not.

Creating a culture of accountability in your company requires far more than making values proclamations that you're an accountable culture. Accountability-capable agreements need to be hard-wired into all deployment tactics. For this to happen, accountability training must be built into personnel training, because most people come to your company with very little understanding of how to construct accountability-capable agreements.

You now have three absolutely vital, yet chronically overlooked, training and tactical keys to Upheavals Literacy and resilience:

1) Self-Responsibility Training
2) Impact Literacy Training
3) Accountability Training

These three skills also form the necessary foundation for creating a high performance, high collaboration, high happiness culture.

Connection Deficits That Limit Collaboration and Engagement

A collaborative culture spells out how to create meaning-ful connection that leads to respect, synergy, and trust. If your culture thrives on competition, which may work in the sales department but will not for the rest of the or-ganization, a culture of looking out for number one pre-vails, and this blocks collaboration.

> TRUST IS A NOUN AND A VERB.
> THE MORE OF THE VERB YOU DO THE MORE OF THE NOUN YOU GET.
> – KEVIN EIKENBERRY

A lack of connection shows up as employee disen-gagement. As you probably know, this is a ubiquitous problem that creates high costs in personnel turnover and customer churn. A disengaged team cannot produce innovation, take risks, function well under pressure, or thrive during upheavals. However, merely addressing employee engagement issues is treating the symptom in-stead of the root cause of employee connection deficits. Most engagement strategies end up looking like bribes and parties. These have fleeting impact at best because they don't address the real issue.

> YOUR TEAM CAN ONLY BE AS COMMITTED TO YOU
> AS YOU ARE COMMITTED TO THEM.

Creating durable team connection goes way beyond the futile team building programs of the past. It requires mutual respect that grows out of admiration for each team member's perspectives, attitudes, and skills. While a team member may trust another to catch them in a back fall (remember that exercise?), it does little to foster ongoing trust in the workplace.

Fixing this starts at the top. An executive team that recognizes, respects, and rewards culturally aligned behavior earns team respect and loyalty. Understanding each other's roles and responsibilities, skills, and insights goes a long way toward building a high-functioning team that respects and honors each other.

Without a connected, highly functioning team, you cannot remain resilient during upheavals, as chaos increases their confusion and causes them to withdraw and disengage. Good luck with that.

The Human Factor in Sequencing

When deciding priorities and sequencing, your culture must include human factors in execution risk. Gone are the days when a manager could issue dictatorial commands and expect unquestioning compliance from a group tasked with innovation and excellence. Automation replaces automaton workers, which frees humans to do what we do best, which is to create, collaborate, and innovate.

This means that before tasks are assigned, connection must exist. Always keep this sequencing in mind: *Connection Before Tasks*. Violating this sequencing is another part of why disengaged employees are sources of unnecessary, preventable upheavals.

> HARNESS THE HUMAN FACTOR:
> CONNECTION BEFORE TASK ASSIGNMENT,
> EMPATHY BEFORE PROBLEM SOLVING.

In like manner, problem solving starts with empathy for all of those impacted by the problem. Recognize team and customer impacts and keep these front and center while you work through challenges, or you'll deal with unexpected and undesired side effects. (Again, this is why building impact literacy into your culture is so crucial.)

Internal Surprise Culture-Driven Upheavals

Employee Lawsuits

Employee lawsuits are an unnecessary and often avoidable drain on corporate resources. They disrupt culture, distract teams, and spawn upheavals.

Many lawsuits can be avoided through solid culture and early intervention with troublesome team members. If you see a pattern of employee lawsuits, discover the root cause of the pattern, and fix that.

External Foreseeable Culture-Driven Upheavals

Lack of Community Regard

Positive community regard yields many tangible rewards. One of the many benefits of an ESG and TBL driven organization is greatly elevated positive community regard. When your community perceives you as problematic, you miss out on these benefits and experience retribution in the form of boycotts, bad press, and so forth.

Some of the constructive outcomes of a positive reputation:

❑ Increased speed of non-customer adoption as the community endorses you over other choices, as seen in positive public reviews

❑ Increased ease in recruiting team members as seen in positive employee reviews on sites such as Glassdoor.com, Monster.com, and Indeed.com

❑ Increased ease of getting PR from local and national media, industry, and association publications.

Your marketing department, or better yet Chief Integrity Officer, should routinely provide you and your fellow executives with public reputation insights. Even a small increase in negative reviews should be addressed rapidly. Make sure that you perform root cause analysis to resolve the source of these. Don't just try to manage the symptoms, or you'll be setting yourself up for more unnecessary upheavals in the future.

External Surprise Culture-Driven Upheavals

Competitive Disruption

When your competition's culture has a higher perceived customer value than yours, you'll experience unexpected upheavals.

Examples include Sears catalog business being usurped by Amazon, Kmart being replaced by Walmart and Target, Nordstrom outliving Nieman Marcus, and Blockbuster being killed by Netflix.

All these companies offered essentially the same products, but the winner delivered non-product differentiation in the form of better customer service, frictionless customer experience, and bringing innovation to the customer.

What non-product, culture-based differentiators do your competitors offer that you don't? What are you offering that they aren't? What can you bring to your culture that your customers admire in ways that create superior value beyond your actual products or services?

Executive Development Upheavals

While we've discussed succession planning for the C-Suite in the companion book, *The Nimble C-Suite*, let's next take a closer look at how the lack of formal executive development procedures set the stage for upheavals.

Lifecycle Impact

All businesses go through lifecycle phases; from launch, to growth, to optimization, to reinvention, to disposition. Each phase requires different executive skills in different development areas. There is no business that doesn't go through change. An executive's most important skill is wrangling change.

At each level of growth, new challenges appear that demand expanded executive cognitive capacity to handle ever-increasing complexity. Many a company has stalled when its growth exceeded the founder's capacity to direct an increasingly complex organization. A founder who is in denial about this, has fallen under the delusion that they have already become who their business now needs them to be. This does far more than only stunting their own growth as an executive. The micromanagement this causes drives away those in the company who have the talent to build future success.

Dealing with Micromanagement

Micromanagement is a clear sign of someone whose responsibilities are beyond their cognitive capacity or executive skills limits. When you notice this, take these steps:

❑ Immediately reduce their cognitive load by lessening their responsibilities and stressors

❑ Simplify, eliminate, and automate tasks to reduce cognitive demands

❑ Train them to better manage complexity through prioritization and triaging skills

❑ Train them on how to make better complex decisions

❑ Provide them with coaching to install these new skills through guided application in day-to-day situations.

Exceeding someone's cognitive capacity can be prevented with continuous executive development, mentoring, and coaching, which installs the skills, insights, and tools required to handle the next level of complexity.

> CHOOSE MENTORS WHOSE HISTORY IS YOUR FUTURE.

Succession Planning

Your experiences and training got you here, bringing a unique blend of perspective and insights, trials and successes. Who has the talent and experience to replace you?

Top executives have their eye on the next in line for each critical post. They have a succession path for each key player, including mandatory mentoring, coaching, and skills training programs. This reduces upheavals from talent loss and talent scarcity. (They also plan with exit options in mind for themselves and the company.)

> IT TYPICALLY COSTS MORE THAN SIX MONTHS' SALARY
> TO REPLACE AN EXECUTIVE.

Given that executive search firms charge one third of a year's salary to find candidates, and that it usually takes 90 days in a new company to be effective, you'll pay the cost of seven months' salary to replace an executive, with overall costs ranging anywhere from 90 – 200 percent, according to the Society of HR Managers.

It's completely worth the far more minor investment of developing your people than the potentially uncontrolled costs of talent replacement and accompanying upheavals.

Perspective Differences

Perspective differences can trigger upheavals, especially when one arrogantly assumes their success in one market or executive position will translate to success in another market or executive position.

> SUCCESS IS A LOUSY TEACHER.
> IT SEDUCES SMART PEOPLE INTO THINKING THEY CAN'T LOSE.
> – BILL GATES

We know of a situation where a highly respected chief marketing officer from a household-name consumer packaged goods company was hired with high expectations by a leading high-tech distributor. She attempted to apply her deeply experienced perspective to the I.T. world and failed miserably, to the deep disappointment of all concerned. Her well-meaning assumptions that I.T. is purchased the same way that household bleach is purchased (based on consumer propensity versus the nature of the mission) completely missed the mark. This thinking error caused upheaval in an otherwise well-functioning organization.

John Sculley came from running PepsiCo to running Apple with mixed results. This another example of perspective mismatch. Steve Jobs reportedly never forgave him for this, even though the hiring error was on the part of Apple not on the part of Sculley.

We've also seen numerous situations where a COO was promoted to CEO, only to realize that their lack of sales experience impeded company growth as they focused on operational efficiencies at the expense of revenue generation.

You can't cost cut your way to success.

That said, it's also possible for a nimble executive to bring success from one industry to a completely different industry when they can adapt their perspective to the new position, instead of trying to adapt their new position to their old perspective.

Be aware of incompatible perspectives and the unforeseen second and third order impacts they can impose. Bring these up proactively, before hiring or promotion decisions are made.

Role-Incompatible Temperaments

Success in each business-critical role requires a certain temperament, or worldview lens, that is unique to that role. This misalignment results in well-meaning people being completely blind to critical aspects of their role, and managers frustrated by their lack of performance.

For example, a detail-oriented person doesn't make a good high-level leader because their obsession with the minutia blinds them to the overall picture; they can't see the forest for the trees. Put them in the right role and they'll succeed and in the wrong role, produce upheaval.

Just because someone has seniority, loyalty, and enthusiasm doesn't make them right for a particular role, no matter how much they (or you) feel they deserve it.

> PROMOTING ENTHUSIASTIC INCOMPETENCE GUARANTEES
> THEY'LL ENTHUSIASTICALLY SCREW IT UP.

An important part of role definition is determining what temperament characteristics are required for success, and auditing for incompatible characteristics. Unless there is clarity about this, an executive will spend massive amounts of time trying inefficiently to switch between inherently incompatible mental modes.

In the relatively rare situations when a role does require mixed characteristics, it's better to offload tactical tasks to an associate.

For example, an executive needs an assistant to deal with critical logistical details, which frees the executive's cognitive capacity to focus on the big picture. A well-trained executive assistant multiplies executive impact, freeing time and energy for highly leveraged activities.

> **A NIMBLE EXECUTIVE HAS MORE ON THEIR TO-THINK LIST THAN ON THEIR TO-DO LIST.**

Under stress, one in a mixed temperament role will revert to their strongest style, regardless of whether that style is most resourceful or not. This limits performance under everyday circumstances and lack of Nimbility gridlocks performance during upheavals.

Because of how vitally important role-temperament matching is, we delve into it in much greater detail in the companion book, *The Nimble C-Suite*.

Misunderstand Leadership Styles

A team member who overidentifies with and insists upon employing a specific leadership style regardless of the situation can exacerbate upheavals. A symptom of this is hero worship of a particular leader, in which, for example, they incessantly quote the leader as a way of not thinking for themselves.

> **IF ALL YOU HAVE IS A HAMMER, EVERYTHING LOOKS LIKE A NAIL.**
> **– ABRAHAM MASLOW**

We discuss leadership styles, when they're useful, and why we suggest against identifying with a specific style, in the companion book, *The Nimble C-Suite*.

Do you have team leaders overidentifying with a leadership style? We bet you do because this is exceedingly common. What will you do to handle this?

The Anti-Nimble CEO

An example of leadership style over identity is the anti-nimble CEO who arrogantly insists on their narrow perspective. They have firmly entrenched *confirmation bias*, where they only seek and believe data that backs their position, and they spin countering facts so these don't threaten their belief. Show them clear compelling evidence that challenges their confirmation bias and they'll discount it as irrelevant, biased, or flawed.

Confirmation bias reinforces blind spots. Everyone else sees the blind spot, but the person with it denies what others see. Leaders, owners, CEOs, executives, and managers with disowned blind spots drive a business into the ground. Even as the company goes up in flames, they are still insisting they are right and that the company – and them – are simply a victim of circumstance.

Inflexibility is the hallmark of an anti-nimble CEO and an unsustainable company.

Leadership Assessment Tool Misuses and Over Dependance

Many organizations use assessment tools to identify strengths, personality, communication strategy, intelligence, etc. While these are useful in screening, most are far from foolproof; a smart person can quickly figure out the "right" answers to give in order to get their desired result.

We've seen assessment tools reject perfectly good candidates because the tool was testing for a skill that isn't needed in the position they would be filling. We've also seen good candidates rejected because they didn't assess well in an area that could have easily been fixed with a little training and coaching.

Assessments must be used in context and interpreted by professionals experienced in applying the results to each unique situation.

Talent Upheavals

As we write this, it's a talent seller's market, with top talent scarce and demanding more to take on a new role. They are reluctant to move, uninterested in lateral moves, and demanding higher compensation packages. You may have noticed that benefits aren't valued like they once were.

The result is that more executive openings are going unfilled longer, and the incoming executive has higher compensation, often greater than the hiring executive. This has been driving compensation increases across the board. Are you experiencing this upheaval?

Nimble executives have a well-conceived talent succession strategy, know how to hire people with execution capacity now and the potential to later occupy roles one to two levels higher, providing that you have a development program and coaching in place that prepares them for greater responsibility.

Do you have talent with the following characteristics:
- ❏ **Depth** – They have deep knowledge of their area of accountability and responsibility, understanding the strategy required and can quickly learn the tactical details needed for solid, resourceful decision.

❑ **Breadth** – They have broad perspective, understand how they fit into the operation, sufficient impact literacy to understand how their decisions impact the rest of the team, and empathy for others' challenges.

❑ **Quality** – They have high integrity, do the right thing even when there is no policy, checks, or balances, are able to communicate clearly, and are able to resolve implementation breakdowns collaboratively. They express a combination of humility and unshakable confidence as appropriate.

❑ **Potential** – They have the cognitive capacity to handle the complexity of the next level or two up the organization. With the right skills development, sage guidance, and coaching, they can become the heir apparent for a higher leadership level.

❑ **Right Placement** – They are in the optimal role for their temperament, experience, and mindset. They haven't been placed because of seniority, but by merit and capability. Their peers respect them and their subordinates seek their wisdom.

Internal Foreseeable Talent Upheavals

Three Nepotism Landmines and Other "Favored Status" Traps

Well-meaning nepotism creates major challenges in many a family business, in non-family businesses where some employees have "favored status," and in friendly mergers where there's an agreement to keep the executive staff employed. Navigating these challenges well is only possible when the prickly problems these situations pose are addressed in psychologically savvy ways.

Here are three of the biggest challenges that should be dealt with proactively when nepotism is in play:

❑ How will everyone who will be impacted resolve the relationship repercussions if a nepotism hire is released? Do you want to go home to your spouse right after you've terminated their brother?

❑ How will nepotism hires be dealt with if they take liberties that you wouldn't tolerate from other team members? Too often nepotism hires and favored status personnel figure that you won't do anything if they do this. How do you handle a sister who's underperforming to the company's detriment while dad is still chairman?

❑ If a nepotism hire or someone with favored status commits fraud, will they be prosecuted the same way that would happen if it was any other employee? What do you do when a child misappropriates your high-limit corporate card for unauthorized extravagant personal purchases?

> ONLY HIRE PEOPLE YOU CAN FIRE AND SUE
> OR YOU'LL BE AT THEIR MERCY.

Treating family employees, or favored status employees, better than other team members triggers personnel resentment and disengagement, sets undesired precedents for bad behaviors, engenders mistrust, and disrupts company culture. This in turn hampers your ability to nimbly avoid and handle upheavals. Double standards are the death knell of company cultures.

Navigating these challenges requires careful consideration, skillful guidance, and sophisticated discussions; you may need external help. Our advice: only employ family members with clear, written agreements on behaviors, boundaries, and consequences. "I've hired you because of what you can do, not because of our family relationship (or friendship). Remember, you can be fired like any other employee." Treat them exactly like an unrelated employee. And ensure that they proactively discuss how personal relationships will be handled if their continuance as an employee were to become untenable.

Internal Surprise Talent Upheavals

Loss of Key Executive

Losing a key executive often triggers upheaval unless they oversee well-executed systems that can continue without their direct attention. If they operate with hidden or undocumented processes, withhold silo-critical information, or are the sole possessors of trade secrets, their unplanned loss can trigger unrecoverable damage.

When there isn't a potential replacement in the wings, transition complications can have negative impacts on your team as well as on investor confidence.

The solution is for all executives to have *escrow packages* in place, which upon their death or departure are released to the appropriate executive. These contain passwords, trade secrets, and other artifacts that allow their successor to start performing from Day One.

What would happen if you lost a key executive? Could your team continue unimpeded or is your inattention to this setting you up for a potential upheaval?

Significant Illness or Death of Key Player

This same principle applies to other key players. Could one of their team members immediately step into their role and assume their responsibilities? What key player succession plans do you and your team have in place?

Competitive Poaching

It's not unusual for a competitor to hire away talent, especially those critical to operations, uniquely skilled, and dissatisfied with their career path or work environment.

While non-compete agreements may limit this behavior, there are many ways to circumvent them, such as being hired into a completely different role that doesn't appear to trigger a sanction, or being hired into a non-competing subsidiary company.

Best case, you'll need to match or better the competitive offer. And if you have to do this, it probably indicates that your current compensation package isn't sufficiently competitive.

Address early warning signs of dissatisfaction immediately. Routinely check on motivational alignment; are they motivated, happy, and fulfilled, in their role?

> FIND REALLY BRIGHT, ETHICAL PEOPLE,
> OVERPAY THEM, AND THEY'LL EARN IT.
> – HOWARD HUGHES

Actively keep up with competitive compensation. While it may seem smart to get a cost advantage from underpaid employees in the near term, the long-term upheavals that result when key members leave usually destroys short-term savings while incurring lasting damage.

Customer Experience Upheavals

In today's customer review-driven world, your happy and disgruntled customers impact new customer choices well beyond your marketing. We believe others' experiences before we believe company marketing that we suspect is self-serving.

When was the last time you bought a new product online without either a personal recommendation or at least checking customer reviews? Hopefully never! When considering trying an unknown restaurant (other than a spontaneous decision while walking down the street), do you first check the on-line reviews? Of course! Since we perceive reviews as generally truthful, we use them to limit the potential of a negative experience. And when we do have a negative experience, how often have we let ourselves off the hook by thinking, "I should have checked the reviews!"

Internal Surprise Customer Experience Upheavals

Loss of a Key Customer

What would happen if a key customer stopped doing business with you? What would happen to your operation? Yes, we know that you've probably considered this. Yet, this is one of the factors we must include in this section for the sake of completeness.

Customer portfolio diversification is a key indicator of business resilience. The general rule of thumb is that if more than 10 percent of your revenue comes from a single customer, you're at risk of upheaval. If this is the case, you have two top priorities. The first is to make sure that you keep a close eye on that customer for any signs of business risk, such as delayed payments, delayed orders, or any kind of negative feedback. The second is to find new business, starting right now.

External Surprise Customer Experience Upheavals

Monitor reviews from every angle: customers, vendors, employees. Actively managing on-line reputation must be an integral part of the feedback process because a string of negative reviews triggers upheavals. Customer, vendor, and personnel experience matters. They are the difference between brand attractiveness and *brand slaughter*.[13]

Who's responsible for managing your on-line reputation with direct feedback to the responsible team members? Who on your executive team do they keep updated? How often does that executive team member keep the entire executive team updated about this?

Business Model Upheavals

Business model upheavals have accelerated because of data-driven automation improvements, enjoyable self-service experiences, and customer expectations of frictionless purchase and delivery. The drive toward sub-

---

[13] See David Corbin's great Wall Street Journal bestselling book, *BrandSlaughter*.

scription models has changed how businesses operate financially and logistically. The old paradigm of guarding cash cows is killing more and more businesses.

Hewlett-Packard printers dominate the market, despite having the highest cost-per-print price point. Why? Their stated goal is to eat their young before their competitors do, by inventing products that obsolete their own models, providing a low cost of acquisition, and making money on consumables.

It's important to always be looking with eyes wide open at sources of external business model upheavals. Dismiss your competitor's market moves at your own peril.

Internal Foreseeable Business Model Upheavals

Change in Ownership

When a company is purchased, the source of funds changes. This can force a change in business models, which creates disruption. See page 114 for more on this topic.

Make sure to examine the impacts of any considered change in capital sources or you're likely to get blindsided by an upheaval you could have prevented.

External Foreseeable Business Model Upheavals

Policy Changes

Government mandates and regulations, industry standard changes, and customer policy changes, also drive upheavals. These can be a surprise if your team doesn't stay up-to-date on external forces.

At the very least, subscribe to services that provide alerts about policy discussions and pending policy changes. Better, have one of your tactical officers monitor these sources of potential upheaval, and regularly discuss these during planning sessions. Devise a plan for addressing both positive and negative impacts.

External Surprise Business Model Upheavals

Societal Crisis

Societal crisis disrupts even the best laid plans, as we've experienced worldwide with COVID. Causes of crisis can include those that emerge organically based on building societal pressures, such as food shortages and toilet paper shortages. They can be triggered deliberately, such as the cancellation of major government-funded projects.

Natural disasters, such as hurricanes and floods, trigger upheavals. This is why large organizations typically operate multiple geographically dispersed data centers, so any loss of mission-critical infrastructure doesn't cripple operations. Another option is to use a cloud company that provides a mirror site that's highly hack resistant, offers comprehensive business continuity and disaster recovery services.

Civil unrest drives upheavals, as illustrated by Target® closing stores after rioters routinely looted certain locations, San Francisco retailers closing stores after legislation relaxed theft prosecution, and the destruction of businesses in parts of Portland, OR.

Your legal department may be able to include contract clauses that release you from obligations in some of these cases, such as termination of leases under unrest situations.

Explore with your executive team how you can anticipate and mitigate the impact of these upheavals to increase your Nimbility.

IP Development and Protection Upheavals

Your intellectual property (IP) creates unique value. Continuous IP innovation and proper protection provides Nimbility and methods to address upheavals.

While this may seem obvious to you, we see a distinct lack of a culture of innovation in many companies, especially those where the founder is distracted by operational issues ("We'll work on innovation after we've fixed these problems"). Or they've decided to relax their focus and enjoy the fruits of their labors ("I've earned it!"), without first handing off responsibility and accountability to a key top-level executive with a full focus on the future and with a highly strategic mindset.

Internal Foreseeable IP Upheavals

Lack of Innovation

If there isn't a continuous stream of innovation in every area of your company, you'll face upheaval. You must innovate at every level: product development, marketing innovation, sales process improvements, customer experience enhancements, infrastructure upgrades, finance and capital strategy, and team skills development. This develops resources for remaining nimble through inevitable upheavals.

Which of these areas have stagnated in your operation? Where do you need to encourage innovation right now or face disruption?

External Foreseeable IP Upheavals

Theft

Rampant piracy dilutes innovation efforts. Which of these protection strategies are you still not implementing, at your own peril?

- ❑ Invent it faster than they can steal it
- ❑ Build IP protection into your products with anti-piracy technology
- ❑ Protect IP as a trade secret – this is one of the best IP protection schemes, used by household names such as Coca Cola's drink formulae, KFC's secret blend of 11 herbs and spices, and Google's search algorithm
- ❑ Aggressively protect IP with legal filings
- ❑ Create and enforce strong non-disclosure and non-compete agreements
- ❑ Aggressively prosecute theft.

Capital Upheavals

Capital upheavals can take the form of investment capital and working capital disruptions.

Internal Surprise Capital Upheavals

Investor Capital Calls

In some private equity agreements, investors can be forced to provide additional capital under certain circumstances. That's never a desirable situation because it drastically affects investor attitude, which in turn often leads to negative impact and upheavals.

Loss or Defection of Key Producer

If a key sales producer leaves, or worse, joins the competition, your working capital may take a hit as revenue declines or is transferred to your competition. This highly disruptive upheaval obviously requires immediate attention.

Create revenue flows that don't depend on a single producer. Decide how much sales execution risk you can tolerate and build the system and team to stay above that threshold.

External Surprise Capital Upheavals

Unanticipated Demand Changes

Unanticipated demand changes happen when a major customer stops buying, or some market force kills sales, resulting in reduction of working capital.

Detect impending changes with ongoing forecasting efforts and market situational awareness. Prepare for the impact with bank credit lines, vendor credit, and cash.

Economic Change

With COVID, the drastic shock on in-person businesses created the greatest economic impact since the end of World War II. You've also lived through many business cycles and world-wide dramas. These won't go away; there will always be a next and a next and a next.

Get better at anticipating these, at preparing for them, and at building your skills to more fully thrive through them.

Infrastructure-Based Upheavals

Any disruption to critical infrastructure that's used to produce and deliver your products will create upheavals. While most companies have well-established contingency plans, it's worthwhile to review your potential points of disruption and decide beforehand how to best mitigate or compensate for these.

Internal Foreseeable Infrastructure-Based Upheavals

Incomplete Security Policy

Your security policy is one of the most important documents in your business because it defines how you'll protect your assets: people, place, data, and customers. It's the source of defining security systems, training, enforcement, mitigation, and post-attack clean up. Without a solid security policy, you're needlessly exposed to risk, not to mention flirting with negligence charges (which may incur triple damages) in the case of disaster.

Security policies must be routinely reviewed to include new technology, new products, and new mandates.

When was the last time your team reviewed your security policy, ideally with a third-party with clearly proven security policy expertise?

Unenforced Security Policy

Without training and enforcement, a policy is useless.

When was the last time you stress-tested your policy by running a simulation to make sure that it's enforced, operational, and optimized?

Lack of Redundancy

Business continuity and disaster recovery are part of your upheaval mitigation insurance. An unnecessary cause of upheaval is data backup failure. Too often these aren't discovered until too late. Any single point of potential failure that is not contingency-planned is an impending upheaval.

When was the last time your data recovery plan was tested? Do you have relationships with backup vendors when a key source gets hit with an upheaval?

Check with your tactical executives on their redundancy and backup strategy, especially about the last time they tested their plan (fail over and revert back cycle), and about how current they are with the latest threats and prevention technologies.

Brittle Systems

Brittleness is the tendency of a system to break under stress or change. Brittleness is low resilience waiting to be crushed by upheavals.

An example of a common brittle system is an I.T. architecture composed of interconnected software vendors. When a vendor updates their software, there's a likelihood of the system breaking. While improved industry standards have reduced this probability, there are still way too many stories of business interruptions when a software patch wasn't correctly tested before deployment.

One major manufacturer has over 10,000 software interfaces. This severely limits any system changes, not to mention their number of cyber-attack points. They do operate a duplicate, clone system just to regression-test software releases before deploying changes to production. However, nothing happens fast in that I.T. system.

While you may be shaking your head in disbelief, companies now average more than 100 (and growing) software applications among all their departments and users. You're probably in a similar situation. Consider the implications in light of what you just read.

While cloud technology increases Nimbility, software interfaces still present points of failure that trigger upheavals, many of which can be avoided or rapidly compensated for, with the right preparation.

External Surprise Infrastructure-Based Upheavals

Utilities Loss

Review the impact of utilities loss on your organization. Consider potential electricity, water, sewer, telecommunications, and other key resource disruptions.

Which of these can you tolerate and where's the breaking point? How will you build greater resilience in light of this?

Better to plan now than deal with an upheaval when your business has ground to a halt and you have no idea of what to do.

Lawsuits

We all dislike lawsuits partly because, far too often, the only clear winners are the lawyers. The best lawyers rarely take a case to court. They instead are masters at negotiating the most favorable outcome instead of facing the arbitrary uncertainty of the legal system.

Lawsuits can come from customers, vendors, the government, a competitor, employees, or even a trade association or guild.

We've observed companies, large and small, with an aggressive policy to distance themselves from vendors and customers who threaten lawsuits. For some, it's a way of doing business, which is a clear red flag. We are aware of companies who have made more money from legal settlements than from selling their own products.

Your legal team is there to protect you from litigation. Have them conduct classes on reducing your legal attack surface. Also identify early warning signals of disgruntled employees, customers, and vendors, and rapidly establish a clear path to resolving their issues in ways that prevent brand slaughter.

If you're experiencing regular legal issues, identify the root causes and address them now, before the situation deteriorates further due to executive inattention.

Process-Based Upheavals

Process change can trigger upheavals. Better companies have careful process change methods. Even so, it's always possible to *lose the recipe*, meaning that what used to work doesn't anymore. This often troubleshoots to an inadvertent change in process, unnoticed vendor changes, or other unexpected factor.

A classic lost recipe story told in engineering circles involves an integrated chip employee who resented having to change out of his protective gear when needing a bio break. This refusal contaminated critical chemistry.

Another classic tail tells of an unexpected computer failure that occurred at the same time every weekday evening. It was caused by a janitor unplugging a cable to access power for the vacuum cleaner. Eyes roll at the I.T. administrator who had thoughtlessly chosen to use a publicly accessible outlet to power mission critical equipment.

Too many people seek shortcut solutions to immediate problems without taking into account any inadvertent expenses of harming ongoing processes. You now recognize this as lack of impact literacy. We suspect these two stories may offer inspiration when solving future challenges.

Internal Foreseeable Process Upheavals

Sequencing Mistakes

Sequencing mistakes happen when implementing new processes without expert guidance. Well-meaning people use their limited experience to make critical choices, usually under stress.

> **THE 2:00 AM SYNDROME:**
> WHAT SEEMS REASONABLE IN THE MIDDLE OF THE NIGHT
> REVEALS OTHERWISE IN THE COLD MORNING LIGHT.

Fix this by having clear policies about decision making methods and by maintaining ongoing oversight of procedure changes that include checks and balances.

Internal Surprise Process Upheavals

Fraud and Theft

You may be wondering why we include fraud and theft under a process category. The reason is that theft and fraud are virtually inevitable when verification systems are non-existent or break down. These upheavals are avoidable more often than not.

> IF THE PAYOFF FOR BAD BEHAVIOR IS HIGH
> AND THE ODDS OF GETTING CAUGHT AND PUNISHED ARE LOW,
> BAD BEHAVIOR HAPPENS EVERY TIME.
> – SCOTT ADAMS

While it's important to trust your team, your customers, your vendors, and your government, it's equally important to have verification processes in place.

The key principle: *trust through verification*. This was the concept behind NCR's first cash register; trust your employees by verifying that what's in the cash till matches the register's recording of purchases. Even though it's been more than a hundred years since the bell rang and numbered flags popped up so that the store owner could visually verify the purchase, you still hear clerks say, "I'll ring you up."

Whether it's stock auditing, waste control, or cameras on the back door, trust through verification.

Where might theft and fraud in your business be going unnoticed because you don't have a verification process in place?

Executive Malfeasance

Fraud and theft can also take the form of bad behaviors by your executive team. Given the opportunity, many will take advantage of systems with verification holes. People with integrity deficits rationalize that if it was important, there would be a policy or check and balance. So, some executives justify malfeasance by saying, "I deserve this, and they can't get rid of me because I'm indispensable, so why not?"

> THE GRAVEYARDS ARE FULL OF INDISPENSABLE MEN.
> – CHARLES DE GAULLE

Sadly, we can't expect altruistic behavior from everyone, so processes and policies must be used to set boundaries that prevent temptation and spell out consequences for misbehaviors.

Executive malfeasance destroys culture and sets the stage for upheavals. If your team can't trust their leaders, they won't follow them into the chaos of upheavals to find the opportunities hidden within them.

Have the courage to impose consequences equally from top to bottom, with no exceptions, even if a departure triggers a temporary upheaval. Forbearance sets negative precedents and this opens the door to future upheavals.

Everyone knows what "...leaving to pursue other interests..." and "...spending more time with the family..." means.

External Foreseeable Process Upheavals

Fraud and Theft

Echoing from the prior section on internal fraud and theft, the same goes for customers, and perhaps more so because there are potentially more customers than personnel, and customers are often less loyal than your team.

Common customer fraud and theft issues include paying short, frivolous loss claims, and misrepresentations.

Warranty fraud can eat up much of a company's profits. One ugly example is swapping parts from broken, out-of-warranty products into newly purchased products and then making a claim. Preventing this requires a system that records product genealogy, a record of serial numbers of subassemblies and even multi-angle photographs used to validate the warranty claim. An additional benefit: you can perform data analytics on failures to proactively identify pending field breakdowns and refine processes, both yours and your vendors'. This is an example of creating a non-product competitive advantage that reduces costs and increases margins.

What are you missing in the way of validation processes that prevent customer fraud? Fill these gaps because they can trigger an unnecessary upheaval.

External Surprise Process Upheavals

Supply Chain Disruptions

In this century we have seen worldwide supply chain disruptions in many iterations: 9-11 halting air traffic, COVID lockdowns, fuel shortages, blocked shipping lanes, a toilet paper shortage, etc. Add your company's experiences to this list. These upheavals impact you and your team, vendors, and customers.

Preventing these requires a backup plan for every logistics aspect of your business. Even if your executive team has these in place, it's still important to routinely review, audit and upgrade these plans.

Where do you have unprotected supply chains?

Operational Reporting Upheavals

A colleague whose entire career centered on corporate turnarounds reported that every situation he faced was triggered by incomplete operational reporting. The executives simply didn't have the indicators necessary to foresee disaster.

When asked why, his answer was, "They were cheap. They didn't want to pay for the necessary systems and tools."

We can't overemphasize the importance of selecting meaningful Key Performance Indicators (KPIs) (or Objectives and Key Results – OKRs) for each critical business function. While profit is a universal indicator of business success, on its own it's not even remotely enough. We discuss KPIs in depth starting on page 122.

Internal Operational Reporting Upheavals

Direction Indication

We advocate KPIs (as well as OKRs) that include leading indicators (predictive), current indicators, and lagging indicators (historic).

In business, the number of sales leads is a leading indicator as is a true sales pipeline report (as validated by customer internal deadlines, not sales team guesses), sales to date and lead quality (percentage of leads that convert to sales in a typical sales cycle) reveal current performance, while profits are lagging indicators.

Without direction indication reporting, you're driving your business through the rear-view mirror and that approach is begging to be blindsided by upheavals.

Anti-Piracy

In over 90 percent of the turnarounds a colleague of ours has handled throughout his long career, he had to eject pirates: those with an intention to steal *from* the company, or to steal *the* company. The way to protect, detect, and eject pirates is through a complete set of unfalsifiable KPIs.

Every key executive must have two to three KPIs that they have full control over, that can't be faked, and that indicate leading, current, and lagging performance. This KPI formula allows rapid intervention for poor performance or malfeasance before their behavior triggers a full-blown, and possibly fatal, upheaval.

Watch for negative trends, unanticipated, or unlikely results because these indicate that further investigation is warranted.

Resource Leaks

KPIs also identify resource leaks, whether unintended or intended. Look for a pattern of stretching time frames, unexpected cost changes, and missed deadlines.

Data Analytics Upheavals

Data analytics is the lifeblood of today's data-driven business. We discuss the Nimbility Data Value Hierarchy, how data increases in value as it ascends to the corporate strategic levels on page 129.

Well-developed data analytics bring unexpected insights to the future and early alerts to problems before they become upheavals. They guide rapid tuning of marketing, offers, prices, and operational performance. Every valuable company has strong analytics that guide strategy and tactics.

Internal Data Analytics Upheavals

External to Internal Data Mismatching

Over time, executives can become overly reliant on data and stop using their discernment to question unexpected results. Just because "the data shows..." doesn't mean that the context is correct, the data are correct, the perspective is correct, or the conclusions are correct. It's easy for confirmation bias to overrule common sense.

> In data science, when one bit of data is suspect, all data are suspect, until they aren't.

Do you use external validation of data analytics to make crucial strategic decisions? When there are discrepancies, how do you resolve them? Can your team freely challenge data analytics reports and conclusions? Which data source is most reliably trustworthy? At what point do you stop trusting a data source? Has the data aged out, that is, it's no longer useful because of when it was gathered?

Internal Politics Upheavals

While it seems that politics are inevitable, that's just not so. A well-lead organization with a culture of communication and collaboration driving to a clear mission minimizes politics.

> CORPORATE POLITICS ISN'T A NECESSITY. IT'S A TOLERATION.

If you tolerate politics, there will be politics. If you ruthlessly root out politics, and you replace it with effective communication and collaboration procedures, you'll attract a world-class team of high performers. Replace politics and you avoid many unnecessary upheavals.

External Political Upheavals

While we have no intention of making this book political, world politics generate more upheaval than in any recent time. With increased civil unrest, uncivil political debate, massive misinformation and dis-information creating confusion and division, and cancel culture pressures, upheavals are constantly coming from new, unexpected sources.

Regardless of your political position, you've been impacted by the politics of your team members, customers, vendors, and the media. Count on this continuing with no end in sight.

Chapter Summary

❑ New market and business forces drive upheavals, which require changes in how you run your company.

❑ Technology advances and generational shifts can trigger avoidable upheavals by actively embracing them.

❑ There are many common sources and cases of upheavals. A savvy executive and their team are aware of them and actively look for ways to mitigate the risks, especially those that are avoidable or can be spotted early enough to manage.

❑ Surprise or unavoidable execution risk factors require resilience and contingency planning to minimize upheavals.

Ask Yourself

❑ What's my strategy for embracing technology change? Where are we behind the growth curve that could trigger an upheaval?

❑ What's my strategy for embracing generational changes? Where are we behind that could trigger an upheaval?

❑ What's my plan for working with neurodiverse people for our benefit and theirs?

❑ How well did I do with the Pending Upheaval Assessment? (See page 42.)

❏ Where do I need to focus to reduce our execution risk? What's my top priority?

Ask Your Team

❏ How well do you think we address new market and business forces as we plan our strategy?

❏ Where do you see us behind the curve in embracing new technology? What's the potential impact of this?

❏ Where do you see us behind the curve in embracing generational changes? What's the potential impact of this?

❏ What do you think we should be doing to better embrace neurodiversity in our team and customers?

❏ Where do you detect unaddressed execution risk? Where haven't we paid attention to this yet?

❏ What do you think is our top execution risk right now? If we don't do something about it, what could be the impact? How would you suggest we begin to address this?

Action Plan

❏ If you haven't, take the Pending Upheaval Assessment starting on page 42.

❏ Ask your key executives to take the Pending Upheaval Assessment.

❏ Based on your assessment, prioritize where you need to focus attention to minimize upheavals and increase Nimbility.

❏ Schedule now to perform the Pending Upheavals Assessment every three months to measure progress and identify potential new execution risks. Ignore this action at your own peril.

Chapter 4:
Upheavals Literacy Maximizes Nimble Strategy Execution

Now that you have a solid overview of the root causes of conflict, challenge, and lack of nimbility, let's explore how to uplevel your skills for maximized strategy execution and minimized execution risk.

You're going to be introduced to *Upheavals Literacy*, the critical skill you and your team require to be nimble. This is the ability to spot and embrace upheavals, giving you the leadership skills and tools to successfully lead through chaos.

Even in good times, nimble execution separates the winners from the losers. A vision, mission, and plan have no meaning or value until they are actualized. Yet, actualizing plans in a meaningful timeframe plagues most companies, especially those headed for upheaval.

> NIMBLE EXECUTIVES HAVE ONE THING IN COMMON:
> THEY GET THINGS DONE IN GOOD TIMES AND BAD.

Master Upheavals Literacy

Upheavals Literacy enables you as an executive to confidently lead through upheavals. Instead of trying to force your existing leadership skills to deal with situations that those skills aren't equipped to handle, it provides you with:

❑ The mindset and skillset necessary for recognizing and upleveling your mental fitness

❑ Tools for successfully navigating the challenges and conflicts in your business

❑ Methods to rapidly innovate and implement to capture the energy of upheavals

❑ Language to articulate your feelings in ways you haven't been able to before and adapt your leadership requirements to the needs of the situation

❑ An invisible competitive advantage that goes way beyond typical product offerings.

> EVEN THOUGH PAIN IS INEVITABLE,
> SUFFERING IS OPTIONAL.
> EVEN THOUGH CHANGE IS INEVITABLE,
> DROWNING IN UPHEAVAL IS OPTIONAL.
> – MARK DIMASSIMO

Who Taught You How to Be Upheavals Literate?

Probably no one. If you're like most leaders and executives, you were trained in the trenches or through ad hoc responses to a specific event, and then applied what you learned in situations where these learnings turned out to not be as useful as you assumed.

If you've been through any leadership or executive development programs, you already know that very few trainers and consultants know how to approach chaos and upheaval in creatively productive ways. You might have found them insistent on their perspective, which happens when they lack the depth to explore options, or when they cling to a set of tactics instead of being freed by a set of principles.

That's why most leaders and executives who must respond to upheavals keep getting knocked down: they lack a complete and systematic way to perceive, prepare, plan, pursue, and profit from upheavals.

Upheavals Literacy is the new superpower for executives who are ready to view the chaotic future as bright and opportunity filled. Leaders with this superpower are sought after, highly valued, and held in deep gratitude for their up-leveled leadership capability.

You too can intentionally become upheavals literate. Are you up for the challenge?

The Nimbility Execution Hierarchy

The ability to get things done during upheavals is the key Upheavals Literacy skill.

The Nimbility Execution Hierarchy builds on proven business leadership principles that you can count on always being effective during stable times and in chaos.

The Hierarchy takes into consideration planning steps and the required team mindset to get the job done. It uses *sequence intelligence* to do the right things in the right order. It asks relevant questions at the right time.

To drive nimble execution, the right elements must be in place before taking the next step, or chaos and upheavals result or get amplified. This becomes your framework for analysis and decision making as a nimble leader. See Figure 5.

```
                    Results

                    Action

                 Intention &
                   Volition

                   Priority

                   Context

                   Objective

                    Culture

            Mission, Vision & Values
```

Figure 5: The Nimbility Execution Hierarchy Defines the Order of Importance for Leadership Focus. Dark Gray Indicates Planning, Light Gray Indicates Mindset.

Each level of the hierarchy must be fully defined and instituted or the foundations of execution crumble. Use this model to help identify where you have potential for upheaval due to over-attention and under-attention.

Notice that between each planning level (dark gray) is a mindset level (light gray). Mindset drives the execution success of the level above it and requirements may change when the level below changes.

In implementing this model, you'll consider the level below and above so that you combine planning and mindset with implementation. E.g., *culture* requires a combination of planning, mindset, and implementation; *action* is about mindset, implementation, and defined results; and *results* are about mindset, planning, and implementation of refinements in action.

Mission, Vision, and Values

A planning level, all success starts with *vision*, defining the big outcome: what's your reason for being and what you want to manifest. This answers these planning questions:

❑ Why do we exist?

❑ How do we create meaningful, substantial impact?

The *mission* is the goal that can be accomplished in the medium term that advances realizing the vision. This answers the questions:

❑ Where are we focused now as our current way(s) of delivering the impact we want to have?

❑ How do we measure success this year?

The *values* define what your company stands for and embodies in accomplishing its mission on behalf of actualizing its vision. Values form the foundation from which emerge guiding principles for decision-making that turns abstract values into aligned actions.

Culture

A mindset level, *culture* establishes how the team *believes* and *behaves* while executing the mission. It establishes what you'll defend with valor, the boundaries of activities and behaviors that define your playing field. It answers the questions:

❑ What do we stand for?

❑ What won't we stand for?

❑ How do we treat each other and everyone else?

❑ What are our guiding principles for decision-making?

Objective

A planning level, *objective* establishes the current set of initiatives to drive toward the mission and therefore the assignments to the strategic and tactical teams. It answers the questions:

- ❑ What do you want to accomplish and avoid?
- ❑ What are we going to do?
- ❑ Why are we going to do it?
- ❑ How does this benefit our team?
- ❑ How does this benefit our stakeholders?
- ❑ How does this benefit our customers?
- ❑ How does this produce competitive advantage?
- ❑ How does this benefit our planet?

Context

A mindset level, *context* considers the emotional, mindset, skillset, and toolset ingredients that will be used to drive outcomes. It includes personal and team perspective, worldview frame, experience, personal culture, resources, history, and state of mind that impacts execution. It answers the questions:

- ❑ What are our available resources?
- ❑ How have we done this before?
- ❑ How can we do this even better or desirably differently?
- ❑ What are our options for solving this?

Priority

A planning level, *priority* is the order or sequence in which you accomplish your objectives. It considers processes and procedures, resources, urgency, and importance. It answers the questions:

- ❑ When are we going to do this?
- ❑ Where are we going to do this?
- ❑ What's the most resourceful sequence to accomplish this?
- ❑ How will we measure success for each step?
- ❑ What are the most useful KPIs for each step?
- ❑ What are we missing?

Intention and Volition

A mindset level, *intention* is the desire to accomplish the prioritized tasks and *volition* is the will and ability for the team to complete the tasks. It answers the questions:

- ❑ What do you expect from this priority?
- ❑ Are all involved able to execute in this sequence?
- ❑ Are all involved ready to execute in this sequence?
- ❑ Are all involved willing to execute in this sequence?
- ❑ How will we determine what's most effective?
- ❑ How can we choose to be most effective over easiest?

Action

A planning level, this determines what specific *action* takes place. Right action cannot take place until all of the lower levels are satisfied; if action occurs prematurely, energy will be spent in activity that is unlikely to deliver the desired results, or that delivers results too late, or delivers at the cost of unintended collateral damage. This answers the questions:

- ❑ Who will take action?
- ❑ How will they take action?
- ❑ How will the results of the action be measured?
- ❑ Who validates the action and results?
- ❑ What desired impacts will this action have?

❑ What unintended negative impacts could this action have, and how will we prevent those from occurring?

Results

This is the outcome of all underlying steps. *Results* are measured with leading and lagging Key Performance Indicators (KPIs), which compare results to the desired outcome. It answers the questions:

❑ Have we accomplished our goal?
❑ How well have we accomplished our goal?
❑ How satisfied are we with the goal now that we see results?
❑ How are we rewarded for producing these results?
❑ How does the team benefit?
❑ How do stakeholders benefit?
❑ How do customers benefit?
❑ How does the planet benefit?
❑ What unintended negative impacts did accomplishing our goal create? How will we repair these, and what will we do differently in the future based on what we learned?

During upheavals, you'll be tempted to wing it. Don't. That's the time when the Nimbility Execution Hierarchy becomes your key tool, keeping you on track during the noise and confusion. Take what you know and work the hierarchy to bring clarity to what needs adjusting and what remains in place. Do this as often as necessary to stay the course.

Use this model and sequence to prevent execution problems, increase Nimbility, and reduce upheavals.

The Law of Wakeup Calls

Upheavals Literacy requires understanding and embracing The Law of Wakeup Calls. The Universe in its wise benevolence, will recycle wakeup calls to an impending upheaval at increasing levels of urgency until the condition gets dealt with. If you keep hitting the snooze button ("this can wait," "this isn't important," "I don't care about this"), the alarm gets louder, and the resulting impact becomes more severe. These wake-up calls start with a simple warning, elevate to a more disruptive caution, and, if unheeded, ultimately escalate to a disaster that cannot be ignored.

You've seen this in the health, relationships, and careers of people you care about. Perhaps in yourself, too.

Wakeup calls are also regularly issued in the corporate world (and the political world), although too often they are only recognized in hindsight after significant and potentially irreversible damage has been done. This can manifest as lost customers, departing key executives, inability to hire good talent, and failed strategic initiatives.

Upheavals are corporate wakeup calls that were ignored at lower levels of intensity and thus got to the point where waking up requires the corporation to go through drastic changes or collapse entirely.

Early Warnings about Impending Upheavals

Part of Upheavals Literacy is being able to detect impending upheavals. How can you detect impending upheavals? To identify yours, truthfully answer the following five questions about yourself and your team.

1. Do You Experience High Turnover of Team or Customers?

This is an indication of blind spots that your team and customers clearly see but aren't being addressed by your management team. Turnover results in unnecessary profit leaks from increased costs of replacing personnel, greater marketing costs to acquire larger numbers of new customers, and the cost of *Brand Slaughter* (as David Corbin calls it) that happens when you relinquish customers to your competition. All of this lays the groundwork for impending corporate upheaval.

2. Do People at All Levels in Your Organization Feel Safe Being Transparent?

Your upheaval detection system must include everyone in your company, as well as your customers and your business partners. Do they feel safe sharing potentially inconvenient or negative news that you need to consider? If not, you have an approaching upheaval that's about to blindside you.

3. Do You Have an *Agree to Disagree* Culture?

This attitude, while seeming to be reasonable, limits everyone's ability to take discussions far enough for truly useful and comprehensive root cause solutions to emerge. Without this the executive team can't choose the priorities based on the company's vision, mission, and values.

Agreeing to disagree is a cop-out that blocks the understandings that are required to avoid upheavals. In *agree to disagree* cultures, all viewpoints appear to be put on the table, but they aren't adequately utilized in multi-dimensional ways. We discuss this further under the topic of the Nimbility Window in the companion book, *The Nimble C-Suite*.

4. Do Your People Seek to See What's Really Happening Outside Their Circle or Do They Cling to Their Information Bubbles (Intentional and Collective Blind Spots)?

Many corporations have cultures with deliberate collective blind spots. This is an engraved invitation to be blindsided by upheavals.

Can you spot the blinders your people have on, individually and collectively? Can you spot your own? Of course not. If you could spot these, they wouldn't be blind spots! Therefore, wise outsiders become vital in helping you see what you and your company can't yet see on your own.

Wise executives have outside coaches or advisors who can discuss any topic of concern and can offer new perspectives that can be inaccessible or seen as non-credible when these come from with an invested team member looking after their career. In contrast, coaches are empowered to tell you things that might challenge your most cherished beliefs or that might result in you having to fire a team member. The best coaches will tell you things – without hesitation – that may get *them* fired.

5. What Aren't People Allowed to Talk About?

One way to quickly identify blind spots is to recognize *don't talk* messages in your organization. "We don't discuss that," or "We don't talk about that," or "We ignore that," are all invitations to be blindsided by upheavals and disruptions.

Ask your yourself and your team:

❑ "What topic taboos do we have in our company?"

❑ "What skills and insights do we lack that have resulted in us making these topics taboo?"

❑ "What risks have we been taking and upheavals have we been courting by banning these topics from discussion?"

How Do I Approach an Upheaval?

Many leaders respond to upheavals *defensively* by doing whatever they can to stop their impacts. They address the symptoms, not the root cause. While symptom control is sometimes temporarily useful for crisis-intervention purposes, it is far from sufficient for thriving. Profiting from upheavals happens by stepping into the center of the chaos, not by trying to avoid it through putting Band-Aids® on the symptoms.

Leaders who thrive in upheavals go on the *offense* by selecting proactive measures that can turn upheaval energy into productive and profitable outcomes.

Nimbility is the ability to rapidly blow past well-understood positions to take advantage of a new situation. Bringing in a small, seasoned team of Nimbilists (those who routinely practice and mentor Upheavals Literacy) can bridge the gap facing executive teams during times of chaos while they master new Nimbility skills.

Let's consider more elements of being upheavals literate.

Positive Expectations

We are a resilient species. We have a long history of surviving enormous upsets, radical technology changes, world wars, and uncontrollable forces of nature. In the

1960s we figured out how to put a human on the moon, and we did it with technology from the lowest bidder. We've solved countless health issues. We've conquered what experts considered impossible.

> WHEN ASKED HOW HE BROKE THE FOUR-MINUTE MILE,
> ROGER BANNISTER OBSERVED,
> "IT'S THE ABILITY TO TAKE MORE OUT OF YOURSELF
> THAN YOU'VE GOT."

Roger Bannister, who broke the declared-impossible four-minute mile, did so while studying medicine, only training three to four times a week during lunch hour, along with recreational hiking and mountain climbing. Near the end of his historic run Roger observed "the tape was receding."

With positive expectations, you can keep your team on track even when it appears the finish line keeps moving.

> IT DOESN'T TAKE MUCH THOUGHT TO BE NEGATIVE.
> – BUCKMINSTER FULLER

This doesn't mean false bravado; it means knowing that your determination is much of the success factor in being nimble. Whether you think you can or think you can't becomes a self-fulfilling prophecy.

Reptile Brain Takeovers and Emotional Self-Management

Distress is the enemy of Nimbility. Situational stress is designed to recruit our inner resources so we can effectively deal with emergencies. Distress is a state of chronic stress. Chronic stress is not merely a health destroyer; it is a creativity and Nimbility destroyer.

Here's why: when we are in any kind of emotionally agitated state (strong fear, anger, sadness, or shame), the midsection of our body manufactures stress chemicals, such as norepinephrine, adrenalin, and cortisol. The impact these chemicals have when they flood our brain is to turn off the thinking areas (cortex) and turn on our limbic system (our Reptile Brain), also called flooding. Our Reptile Brain's response repertoire includes only four options: fight, flee, freeze (deer in the headlights), and faint (play 'possum, hoping the threat will pass without paying attention to us).

Have you ever tried to have a rational thoughtful conversation with someone when their thinking brain is turned off and they are in the midst of a Reptile Brain takeover? Have you ever tried to do strategic analysis and problem-solving while your Reptile Brain is the boss of you? These are fool's errands.

Even so, very few businesses or leadership training programs teach people Reptile Brain Mastery – the skills necessary to remain untriggered, to recognize when you or someone else are triggered, and to restore wellbeing as rapidly as possible. The most you'll usually see is stress management or mindfulness programs. However, the vast majority of those programs teach symptom control and cognitive tricks, not full Reptile Brain Mastery.[14]

Willingness

The superpower of any soldier going into the upheaval of combat is the willingness do something new, to take a confident-even-if-not-fully-certain step forward, and to fail forward as rapidly as possible.

> CONFIDENCE COMES NOT FROM ALWAYS BEING RIGHT
> BUT FROM BEING WILLING TO BE WRONG AND TO ADJUST.

Not everyone is willing. They may be held back by fear of failure (or a Reptile Brain takeover), which means they've already failed. They may be blocked by their paradigm attachment disorder, "This can't work because I've never seen it work" or "I won't know who I am if I shed my familiar paradigm, and that is too terrifying to try." They may be hampered by needing certainty (*tensions competence* deficits), which of course is impossible other than having confidence in one's ability to successfully explore, fail forward, and innovate. Or they may be crippled by chronic distress.

---

[14] Beyond the scope of this book, we have Reptile Brain Mastery and Tensions Competence training programs and can also make other recommendations.

> THE ONLY THING THAT MAKES PEOPLE AND ORGANIZATIONS GREAT
> IS THEIR WILLINGNESS TO BE NOT GREAT ALONG THE WAY.
> THE DESIRE TO FAIL ON THE WAY TO REACHING A BIGGER GOAL
> IS THE UNTOLD SECRET OF SUCCESS.
> – SETH GODEN

Become willing to venture into the chaos in an untriggered state (i.e., not in Reptile Brain takeover), so you can emerge with the prize. Think of the excitement of a new roller coaster ride, not the dread of an IRS audit.

Focus on the Important before the Urgent

Dynamic changes can create confusion that clouds clarity. You'll be tempted to pay attention to the squeaky wheel demanding your focus, the urgent calls for answers right now.

Urgency is driven by a third party's demands, not yours, often by those in chronic distress (Reptile Brain takeovers), who are demanding a panacea for their headaches at the cost of understanding the root cause of what's creating them.

Identifying what's important, a path through the upheaval, and what's urgent, a balm for the upset and uncomfortable, lets you separate the effect from the cause.

You need determined focus to understand the situation and innovate to convert it into benefits. This focus isn't easy and requires a concerted and coordinated team effort fueled by certain skills and dedicated personal power (aka personal discipline).

Have a Destination, Even If It's Temporary

Nothing happens without a goal and a deadline. The nimblest executive team can't act without a target. Give your team something to do that yields insight, increases clarity, and reveals the next step after that one.

> A JOURNEY OF 1,000 MILES STARTS WITH A DESTINATION,
> AND THEN THE FIRST STEP.

Practice doesn't make perfect – it makes progress. Incremental progress matters. You can drive thousands of miles in the dark seeing only a few hundred feet into the future, and that's usually enough to avoid an animal on the road and find a rest stop.

You can alter the destination as you gain more insight and perspective through each step forward, and your team will follow if they have a rationale for the change.

Try it! "Let's go exploring!"

Good Enough Beats Perfect

Nimbilists know that directional accuracy beats perfect decisions. The best analogy for this is sailing. A sailboat is fully on course only for split seconds. The vast majority of the time, the boat is moving to the left or right of its ultimate destination in order to make best use of the wind. While the intended direction of the journey remains clear, it is almost always off course on the way there.

Making progress matters, no matter if you're detoured or must make rest stops.

> IF YOU ARE NOT EMBARRASSED
> BY THE FIRST VERSION OF YOUR PRODUCT,
> YOU'VE LAUNCHED TOO LATE.
> – REID HOFFMAN

Instead of being bogged down by perfection, celebrate incremental wins, incremental profits, and incremental learning.

Humility

This is your ability to move focus from your own preconceptions to others who hold the insights, perspectives, and innovative mindsets that can reveal new answers that you can't yet see. The antidote to many blind spots, humility isn't about thinking less of yourself, but rather actively expanding your awareness to understand and honor other perspectives that unlock untapped mental resources.

Humility requires admitting that you're on a path to understanding along with everyone else on the team. You'll learn as you go, with each directionally correct choice illuminating the path to the next correct choice toward mastering your upheaval. You're failing forward.

> I HAVE NOT FAILED, NOT ONCE.
> I'VE DISCOVERED TEN THOUSAND WAYS THAT DON'T WORK.
> – THOMAS A. EDISON

This is how all great, intentional invention happens. Every attempt by Thomas A. Edison to create a successful electric light filament led to the next attempt until he reached success in 1879, with his electric light ultimately unraveling the market for kerosene that had been dominated by John D. Rockefeller. Instead of clinging to Paradigm Attachment Disorder about kerosene, Rockefeller nimbly pivoted to produce gasoline, which in turn allowed Henry Ford's Model T to replace the horse and buggy, and this drove the replacement of the village blacksmith with the filling station.[15] Upheavals beget upheavals, which is why Upheavals Literacy is so important.

Blind Spot Busting

A critical skill in Upheavals Literacy is the self-discipline to suspend judgement until you illuminate blind spots and address unheeded wakeup calls which begins a journey to a new desirable outcome.

> IGNORING A RED FLAG WON'T MAKE THE DANGER SAFER.

Creating a culture of respectful *blindspotting* increases nimbility. Rather than pointing out blind spots as a passive-aggressive attack method, blindspotting is instead used to genuinely identify what you and your team don't know that you don't know. We discuss how to do this on page 19.

It's a Reptile Brain mistake to view a new perspective as a personal threat or challenge to understanding. If you feel challenged, take a breath, and master your Reptile

---

[15] Between 1908 and 1927 Henry Ford sold 15 million Model T cars, forever transforming transportation. In the U.S., 200,000 filling stations opened between 1905 and the end of the 1920's.

Brain's impulse to react. Once you're again untriggered, choose to use the situation to improve yourself and your team. Don't worry about whether the intentions of the person challenging you are to improve you or disapprove of you.

That said, however, truly trustworthy sources always seek improvement, even if it's something as seemingly small as pointing out a verbal tic (such as, "You know", "Like...", "Right?") that's impeding professional communication flow.

Blind spots are human. They are what we don't see in ourselves, others, or situations, that undermine our well-being, relationships, success, and positive impact. Here is the most important thing to remember on your journey toward *Blindspotting Mastery*: Others usually see our blind spots more easily than we do, just as we usually see other people's blind spots more clearly than they do. We can either use blind spots to beat up each other (and ourselves) or we can become *Blindspot Curious*.

Positive psychology while useful, tends to focus so much on the brighter side of things that it typically does not include training in becoming adept at Blindspotting within ourselves and in service to others.

Providing yourself, your fellow executives, and your personnel, with Blindspotting Mastery Training is just as important as providing Reptile Brain Mastery Training.

Perspective

What differentiates upheavals from other business cycle impacts is that upheavals include a barrage of new, unexpected, unanticipated factors that can easily become overwhelming. We explore these factors in detail starting on page 37.

New and broadened perspectives increase options. You may have had a few epiphanies reading this book which have brought you new perspective and new options.

AN EPIPHANY IS A SUDDEN FLASH OF INSIGHT
THAT MAKES SENSE OF THE PAST
AND BRIGHTENS THE FUTURE.

Accessing perspectives from those who are upheavals literate sparks new insights, lets you sort out the root causes, and capitalizes on opportunities hidden within upheavals. If you think we can help, let's talk because exploring perspectives is our favorite activity. Learn more on page 199.

How to Find Your Place In an Upheaval

Upheavals happen when people have insufficiently defined roles of accountability and responsibility that equip them to proactively detect sources and avenues of upheaval.

A LACK OF RESPONSIBILITY UNLEASHES THE WORST IN US.
– KEVIN KELLY

In a world where messengers of the truth regularly get shot, few with corporate career goals are willing to discuss key issues unless the leaders and the culture

make it safe to be a proverbial *canary in the coal mine.*
Are you willing to step into this role?

The bottom line is this: capitalizing on upheavals requires wise, sage, yet nimble, leadership that provides clearly defined universal principles, simple systems, and executive-level mindsets and skillsets that develop Upheavals Literacy.

One Solution

Our consulting firm, NimbilityWorks, catalyzes the emergence of corporate leaders into sagehood by equipping and facilitating them to transmute upheavals into wisdom generators that elevate their business success along with their personal legacy.[16]

We make sure you don't hustle through your upheaval so quickly that you leave massive amounts of untapped gold behind. Sages don't leave the *dark night* of upheaval prematurely; they first fully extract the offered wisdom.

We help you eliminate negative emotional charges (Reptile Brain Takeovers) and blind spots about your situation, so you can step into gratitude for your upheaval's gifts without needing to keep repeating the pattern that led to the upheaval. We facilitate you in allowing upheavals to do their magic, so you emerge from them with greatly enhanced Upheavals Literacy.

---

[16] Learn more on page 199.

Chapter Summary

❑ Upheavals Literacy, the ability to spot and address upheavals, is a key skill for you and your team to be nimble.

❑ The Nimbility Execution Hierarchy guides you to the correct sequence in building your execution plans during good times and in upheaval.

❑ The Law of the Wakeup Calls describes the early warning signals of upheavals. Understanding this is part of Upheavals Literacy.

❑ Upheavals Literacy includes being alert to early warnings about impending upheavals.

❑ Learning how to approach upheavals for maximum benefit increases Upheavals Literacy.

Ask Yourself

❑ What's my level of Upheavals Literacy? Where are my gaps and how will I fill them?

❑ What's my leadership map? How can the Nimbility Execution Hierarchy supplement or uplevel my process?

❑ What wake up calls have I been ignoring? What might be the impact of me continuing to ignore them?

❑ What wake up call takes top priority for me?

❑ Where are the gaps in my team's Upheavals Literacy? What could be the impact if I don't address this sooner rather than later.

Ask Your Team

❑ How well can you spot upheavals before they happen? Where do you detect a gap in these skills? What would it be worth to fix that?

❑ How well can you address upheavals when they happen? Where do you detect a gap in these skills? What would it be worth to fix that?

❑ Where have you detected a potential upheaval that we continue to ignore? What could be the impact if we don't address it sooner rather than later?

❑ If you could uplevel your skills around Upheavals Literacy, what might that mean to you, your team, and your career? What if we don't?

Action Plan

❑ Identify the value of upleveling your Upheavals Literacy. Identify the cost of not doing so.

❑ Identify the value of upleveling your team's Upheavals Literacy. Identify the cost of not doing so.

❑ Create a prioritized plan for addressing and upleveling your company's Upheavals Literacy.

❑ Make this training part of your on-boarding process for new employees.

❑ Measure the impact of this training on the decrease of upheavals and the increase of well managed upheavals.

Chapter 5:
Business Essentials
That Bring Nimbility

In this chapter, we discuss the business elements required to nimbly run a business in today's world. This sets the scene for you to discuss roles and responsibilities with your executive team and your tactical team. Complexity reduction starts at the top; simplicity implementation starts at the bottom.

While you probably know much of what we'll cover in this chapter, we have included this so we have a common vernacular that enables us to more easily make your team nimble. Along the way, you may have a few epiphanies.

Clear Vision and Specific Mission

Every organization has a vision and mission statement. Vision is the destiny that the company desires to manifest. (Mission is what they provide to bring that vision about.)

Yet most vision statements are fuzzy and general; they could be mixed and matched with almost any competitor's declarations or website. The solution to this is to convert your mission and vision into a customer-centric action statement. For instance...

{ 113 }

From: "To bring leading-edge technology to market, empowering our customers to be more productive and competitive."

To: "We're the team that teaches our customers how to better run their company, helping them see a new and better way of doing business with relevant technology."

To make your statements distinctively compelling requires describing the desired attitudes, behaviors, and goals for your team.

"We believe that learning and the quest to understand our customer never ends because we know more about our products, our customers, and our competitors, than anyone else."

Include a description of what happens when things go wrong.

"We hate telling our customers 'no' to a reasonable request. We'll find the answer, make it right, or find someone else who can do it. No excuses. We say, 'I know who knows that. I'll arrange for you to connect.'"

Can your team articulate your vision and mission without referring to the written statements? If not, rewrite them to be inspiring, meaningful, memorable, and actionable.

Business Models are Set by Funding Sources

The source of funding and ongoing revenue determines an operation's business model and therefore its Nimbility.

Models vary depending on whether the investment comes from Wall Street, venture capital, angel investors, the government, or friends, family, and fools. The business model depends on whether revenue comes from taxes, tuition, transactions, subscriptions, deposits, or donations.

Think about your sources of funding. How are they impacting your business decisions? Are upheavals being caused by your capital sources? Is your capital enabling or limiting Nimbility?

As time passes and upheavals occur, what's considered valuable, worthwhile, and profitable changes, and this forces a re-engineering of an organization's business model.

Here's how the Nimbility Business Model Cycle works:

- ❑ The *funds source* determines the *business model,*
- ❑ Which is defined by *business rules* and *corporate structure,*
- ❑ Which get implemented through *I.T. deployment,*
- ❑ Which supports and augments *executive and team business acumen* and operations,
- ❑ Which determines the *customers and revenue,* who does business with the company and how much they buy,
- ❑ Which rewards the funds source with a return on investment,
- ❑ All of which is supported or disrupted by *culture.*

That's a mouthful, but it's a complete picture. Re-read it until you get it. See Figure 6.

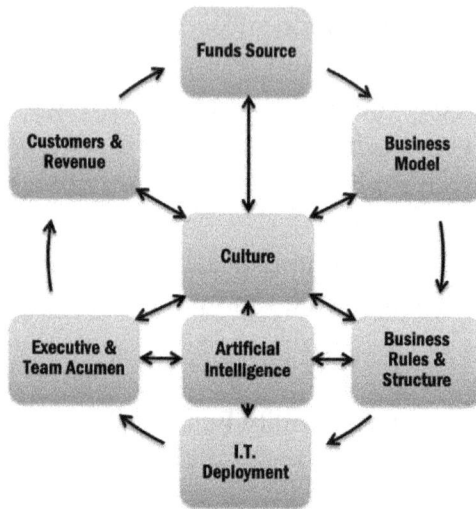

Figure 6: The Nimbility Business Model Cycle

The business model determines the required level of the team skill and executive acumen and brings automation and self service to customers who insist on instant service. For example, have you ever talked to a human while shopping on Amazon, other than to thank the UPS® delivery driver? We order food and it arrives at our doorstep. Expect more of this in the future. And expect the public to expect more of this in the future.

Your I.T. deployment can automate and enforce business rules and can broker exceptions. For example, a fast-food restaurant model allows unskilled workers to crank out the food and take money, but they can't refund money without a manager override.

A franchise owner licenses a proven business model that doesn't require them to have experience or acumen in that market. If they follow the process, there's a high probability of success.

Conversely, a business model that requires a high degree of team and executive cognitive capacity – such as specialized consulting (legal, medical, technology, architecture, engineering) – may not be highly scalable unless artificial intelligence defines the business rules.

All of this centers around the organization's culture, which can be set by the business model and which can override any of the business model elements. Get the culture right and everything in the model flows. Get it wrong and your culture will break your business model.

> IN EVERY BUSINESS, THE SOURCE OF FUNDS
> DICTATES THE BUSINESS MODEL
> AND CULTURE DICTATES THE MODEL'S SUCCESS.

While defining and managing culture is beyond the scope of this book (yet well within our wheelhouse), understanding its impact on business models and resulting business success brings maturity to business model development.

Where Does Artificial Intelligence Fit In?

With the introduction of *artificial intelligence* (AI) and *machine learning* (ML), new, complex business rules can be identified and incorporated into I.T. deployment. AI training comes from watching encounters, successful and unsuccessful, to extract complex sets of factors present in an interaction. Current AI tools require about 70,000 encounters to accurately determine new business rules and recommendations.

A good example: every time you search Amazon®, AI makes suggestions based on what others purchase, along with relevant paid ads. Their AI algorithms have become so precise and reliable that Amazon is now the default search engine for buyers. As we write this book more than six in ten purchase searches start at amazon.com.

IBM's AI platform, Watson®, has been used for cancer diagnosis and treatment recommendations, although with mixed reviews. In a complex scenario such as this, we'd expect the AI ultimately to out-diagnose physicians and for the doctors to push back in self-defense. Eventually, AI will become the preferred first-opinion health diagnosis platform, especially as the complexity of medicine continues to grow exponentially and treatment options expand at a breathtaking pace.

ARTIFICIAL INTELLIGENCE IS ONLY AS GOOD AS HOW IT'S TRAINED.

We also want to caution you that AI can unintentionally take on unexpected culture consequences as it can learn bad, unresourceful behavior as easily as it can learn good, resourceful behavior.

The punch line: AI-generated business rules always require executive review to ensure that your ethics and your culture remain intact. Do you have a system in place to regularly audit this?

Wall Street Drives Business Models

Wall Street drives publicly traded company business models. Investors reward certain models with stock valuation beyond common earnings per share ratios, so corporate executives select models most likely to raise the value of their stock.

> CAPITAL ISN'T STUPID. IT MOVES TO WHERE IT CAN EARN A RETURN.
> – BRUCE WUOLLET

The biggest valuation lever today: moving from transactional revenue to recurring revenue because stock valuations typically increase by two to six times when you do. We've seen drastically higher multiples with Amazon and other business unicorns (Uber®, Snapchat®, Instagram®, etc.). If your company doesn't generate recurring revenues, investors will become less and less interested in it. This effect is driving every modern business model pivot.

> THE BIG BUSINESS MODEL SHIFT: RECURRING REVENUE.

When building recurring revenue, the strategy shifts to one that commoditizes transactional competitors and creates unique value through continuous focus on elevating customer outcomes. This is driving the transformational economy.

Business Rules Implement Business Models

Business models get installed in an organization through business rules. Need to change the model? Change the rules.

Rule changes often demand changes to I.T. deployment, data flow, and decision trees. New rules change the information required by executives to drive the business and change how customers interact. The more dynamic the business model, the more dynamic the changes in business rules, challenging traditional I.T. architecture inflexibility. Inflexible I.T. systems limit Nimbility and introduce system brittleness: the tendency for the system to break when stressed or changed. This must change, driving new I.T. strategies and tactics.

Customer Business Model Transformation

We've experienced a radical shift in consumer expectations driven by mobile devices, the Internet, and social media.

> MARKET WINNERS DELIVER
> A FRICTIONLESS EXPERIENCE
> TO PASSIONATE CUSTOMERS.

Customers want everything right now. They want a frictionless customer experience as delivered by Uber for transportation, by Amazon 1-Click® for every imaginable purchase, by Netflix for entertainment, and by voice command to Alexa®, Cortana®, and Siri®.

We used to travel to an office to work because that's where the network to the data center terminated and where the landline phone attached to our desks.

Now IP telephones route calls to where we happen to be and most people just carry a mobile phone. With the elimination of long-distance phone bills, your area code no longer indicates anything other than where you first bought your mobile phone.

> WE NO LONGER GO TO WORK, WE JUST DO WORK.

We can access virtually any digital tool with ubiquitous broadband Internet access, which means just about anywhere there's a Starbucks® or Panera®, cellular coverage, or where we can aim a satellite antenna. We can easily work virtually. Millennial workers function well in virtual teams thanks to countless hours of on-line gaming, collaborating to solve complex problems with people they've never met in person.

This means we no longer care about the data center location because we can access it from everywhere. I.T. location becomes irrelevant, so let's put data centers where we can get the cheapest land and power. Better yet, just push the computing requirements to the customers' personal device and operate the corporation out of the cloud. Yes, there are exceptions to this, yet very few.

Therefore, unless customers feel a need to show up at a physical location to purchase goods or consume services, businesses no longer need much (if any) dedicated office space. You see this trend reflected in a falling demand for commercial office space and increasing retail vacancy.

> ALL BUSINESS MODELS EVENTUALLY DIE.
> – JEFF BEZOS

How has your business model adjusted to the changes of your customers' business model or lifestyle demands? If you haven't adjusted it and aren't continuing to do so, you can expect impending upheaval.

Key Performance Indicators Increase Nimbility

No doubt, you have a dashboard of key performance indicators (KPIs), key results indicators (KRIs), or objectives and key results metrics (OKRs). You use these to determine where to focus management attention, hold your team accountable, and support critical decisions.

Properly established, measured, and reviewed KPIs help you confidently direct the company, identify theft and piracy, signal potential upheavals, and point to resource leaks.

Let's now take a look at how to best make KPIs work to increase Nimbility.

Select Meaningful KPIs

When architecting systems, each procedure (a tactical task) has its set of KPIs, each process (a sequence of tactical tasks) has its set of KPIs, and each system block (a set of related processes) has its set of KPIs. All of these roll up into the overall system KPIs that measure success against the mission.

> WHAT GETS MEASURED, GETS MANAGED.

Tactical KPIs have more granularity and strategic KPIs deliver broader insights. Data quality, data age, and data quantity matters. Don't make a decision based on a single data point; decide how many points you need for a clear indication. When a KPI seems anomalous, first question the data quality, age, and quantity or you may be tricked into a faulty decision, triggering an unnecessary upheaval.

All KPIs Must Roll Up

Every KPI must roll up the command chain; every lower level KPI must inform a higher level KPI. This allows you to drill down into a KPI all the way to the root cause. A dead-end KPI that doesn't roll up may be useful to an individual but becomes useless to management and executives as a performance indicator and troubleshooting tool. It may become invisible, so triggers a needless blind spot.

KPIs Have a Timeframe

KPIs can be classified as leading, current, or lagging indicators. For example, in a car, distance to empty is a leading indicator of future performance, speedometer indicates current performance, and the odometer indicates past performance. A navigation system gives remaining distance and estimated time of arrival as leading indicators, compass heading and speed as current indicators, and time in route and average speed as lagging indicators.

Each area of your company needs all three types of indicators. If you're only relying on lagging indicators, you've got many blind spots that will result in you being blindsided by upheavals.

KPIs Can't Be Manipulated

When choosing KPIs, make sure that they can't be faked or manipulated. Data sources must be auditable and out of the control of the KPI-responsible person. If the KPI numbers seem suspect, consider them as such until you've followed the audit trail and are satisfied that they haven't been spoofed.

Choose Qualitative and Quantitative Indicators

Some KPIs can be generated by measuring, collecting, and processing data for a quantitative result, such as how much cash is in the bank account or how many units were built and shipped today. These are objective dimensions; we all can agree on the measurement method, independently arrive at the same results, and have a third party confirm them through an audit.

Other KPIs are qualitative, turning what can't be physically measured into a metric, such as using a scale of one to ten to rate your personal energy level, a customer's satisfaction level, or an employee's engagement level. These are subjective measurements with different outcomes depending on personal choice, potential confusion about the scale (is 1 good or bad?), and the criteria they use to differentiate, for example, a 2 from a 3.

As an example of this, consider one of Mark's audience members who told him, "Your speech was the best I've heard. I rated you a four and not a five, because only God is perfect." Mark felt honored.

For this reason, when measuring qualitative factors, we strongly recommend using statements measured with an anchored scale where the number is defined. For example: "I'm happy." 1 – Disagree. 2 – Somewhat Disagree. 3 – Not Sure. 4 – Somewhat Agree. 5 – Agree.

A common qualitative measurement is the pain scale used by medical practitioners, shown in Figure 7. Notice the scale is *anchored*, that is, there is a definition for what each point means or measures.

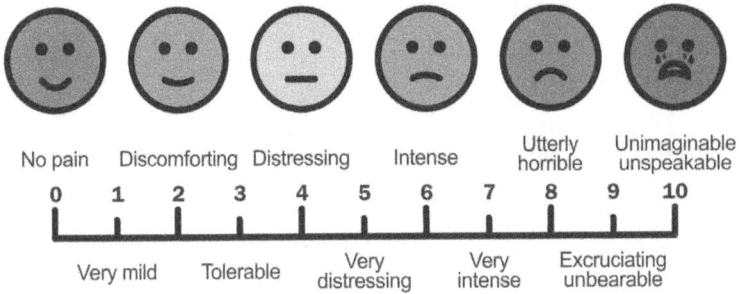

Figure 7: The Pain Scale Used by Medical Practitioners Illustrates a Qualitative Measurement on an Anchored Scale

Whether a KPI is qualitative or quantitative, keep the data source in mind when considering your perspective and interpreting decision impact.

How Many KPIs?

It's possible to have too many KPIs. When this happens, they tend to get ignored or they require unnecessary overhead and excessive time to report.

Take a close look at your KPIs for usefulness and necessity. Eliminate the extraneous and implement the critical.

Leading (Predictive) Indicators

To illuminate the future, select leading indicators for all critical functions. Falling leading indicators warn of potential problems and rising leading indicators alert to a potential need to increase delivery resources. For leading indicators, data age matters. You don't want to be making future-impacting decisions based on aged data.

Examples of leading indicators:
- ❑ Number of new customer leads
- ❑ Sales pipeline details
- ❑ Order size trends
- ❑ Maintenance fee renewal trends
- ❑ Customer satisfaction trends
- ❑ Lost customer trends
- ❑ Manufacturing capacity trends
- ❑ Inventory trends
- ❑ Vendor delivery time trends
- ❑ Cash flow trends
- ❑ Employee overtime trends
- ❑ Employee satisfaction trends
- ❑ Executive satisfaction trends.

How well do your existing KPIs help you foresee the future? Where do you need to identify and deploy them to reduce potential upheaval?

Current (Tactic Choice) Indicators

Current KPIs indicate how you're doing in the moment – your current state – usually indicating a velocity or location parameter. This indicates what process strategy you'll choose (parallel, sequential, outsourced, etc.) if you need to increase or decrease a current measurement.

This type of KPI is useful when you wish to hit a specific daily or weekly goal.

Examples of current indicators:
- ❑ Daily inbound new customer calls
- ❑ Daily sales calls
- ❑ Daily sales quotes issued
- ❑ Computer system up and secure
- ❏ Cash in the bank

❑ Accounts receivable aging
❑ Compliance against mandated deadlines
❑ Daily manufacture output
❑ Weekly task completion.

How well do your existing KPIs help you measure your current state? Where do you need to identify and deploy them to reduce potential upheaval?

Lagging (Historical) Indicators

Lagging KPIs document history, where you have been. This is useful in measuring performance against longer-term goals.

Examples of lagging indicators:
❑ Profit
❑ Growth
❑ Customer satisfaction
❑ New customers year over year
❑ Lost customers year over year.

How well do your existing KPIs help you consider history? Where do you need to identify and deploy them to reduce potential upheaval?

Align KPIs with Vision and Mission

Examine your KPIs for alignment or misalignment with your vision and mission. If they're misaligned, your team is determinedly heading the wrong destination and you can't hold them responsible for that.

Any change in vision, mission, business model, or policy requires a review and realignment of KPIs.

Strategy Sets KPIs Which Focus Strategic Leader Lenses

Each of your executive team has KPIs to measure their performance. These KPIs determine if they keep their job. When the KPI is okay, they stay. If the KPI is low and stays low, they go, right now. We discuss KPIs for specific executive roles in the companion book, *The Nimble C-Suite*.

This means they'll use their KPIs as their decision-making lens. Does this decision support a healthy KPI measurement? If not, they'll say no.

> WHEN YOU GAUGE STRATEGIC PLAYERS WITH TACTICAL MEASURES, YOU FORCE THEM TO BEHAVE TACTICALLY.

We see problems when executive KPIs aren't aligned with their role, such as forcing tactical measurements on strategists. If an executive's KPI is truly tactical, then they need to be part of the T-suite, the tactical team, because their inherent tactical lens will introduce counterproductive tension into the necessary strategic lens of the S-suite. (The S-Suite and T-Suite make up the C-Suite in our new organizational design.)

An example of this is the traditional role of the Chief Information Officer, where their KPI is system uptime and security, both tactical measurements. No wonder why strategic behaviors are rare from a CIO.

Could your executive team's tactical KPIs be hampering their strategic performance?

The Nimbility Data Value Hierarchy

With data being centric to the modern business model, it's the source of your KPIs. So, let's now take a closer look that brings a more useful perspective on how to consider data as you lead your nimble executive team.

There are three fundamental roles when dealing with data: *curators*, *creators*, and *consumers*. At each level, the value of the data increases by at least an order of magnitude with a commensurate increase in supporting budgets. See Figure 8.

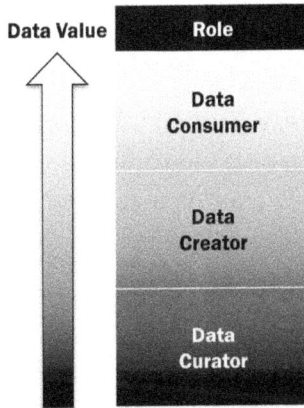

Data Value ↑ | Role
Data Consumer
Data Creator
Data Curator

Figure 8: Nimbility Data Value Hierarchy —
Data Value Increases as It Moves Up the Hierarchy
from Curators to Creators to Consumers

Let's dig into each of these levels.

Data Curators

Data curators live in the data center and are concerned about data security, system manageability, data compatibility across databases, and data availability – keeping the bad guys out and not making it too difficult for the good guys to access data when and where they want. Their job is to *maintain* the data systems and *manage* the data.

Do the data curators care about the data?

DATA CURATORS SEE NO VALUE IN THE DATA.

No! They couldn't care less about the data. They don't care if it's candid pictures of cats or the cure for cancer; it's all the same to them. They care about the data integrity but care not about the data themselves.

As long as the data they are tasked to oversee is secure and available, so is their job and career. But if the system goes down or is compromised, their career is on the line. If the issue isn't resolved and cleaned up quickly, their career options default to The Geek Squad® or selling I.T.

You're laughing because it's true.

Yet, most of the recent advances in I.T. (big data, flash storage, mobile devices, XaaS[17]) go way beyond the data curation realm, providing new business value to the C-suite and tactical implementers. The vast majority of these value propositions are lost on the I.T. department. These innovations become more of a threat than a benefit to CIOs because of potential operational disruption and system downtime triggered by new, unknown technology.

---

[17] XaaS denotes *Something as a Service*, whether software, hardware, infrastructure, etc. which provides flexibility, rapid deployment, and usage-based pricing.

Why Digital Transformation Stalls

This is why most digital transformation initiatives don't go well. They are led by the most conservative, change resistant department heads who are threatened by transformation, concerned for their career, and usually have great difficulty seeing the benefits of the new paradigm.

Typically, data curation only extends to the systems that the data center owns or leases. Anything that the CIO doesn't specify, fund, or control they disparagingly call *shadow I.T., rogue I.T.,* or *stealth I.T.*

> SHADOW I.T. EXISTS WHEN
> THE NEEDS OF THE COMPANY CHANGE FASTER
> THAN THE ABILITY OF THE CIO TO RESPOND.

Digital transformation negatively impacts the data curation team because of their inability to keep up and figure out how to manage rapid change and new technologies. These are the people being displaced by I.T. upheavals.

What Data Curators Want: Visibility to Manage

Data curators want to feel safe and want to be able to *manage* the data to bring more value to the curation system that they've architected. See Figure 9.

Data Value	Role	Requirements	Result
	Data Consumer		
	Data Creator		
	Data Curator	Security Manageability Compatibility	Visibility Flexibility Job Security

Figure 9: Nimbility Data Value Hierarchy Data Curator Strategy — Visibility into the I.T. Ecosystem to Manage Data Anywhere

Data Curator Business and Nimbility Risk

The new key to solid uptime service level agreements (SLAs) in mixed systems: *visibility* into the operations of the entire I.T. ecosystem.

When an end user doesn't get the data they want, when they want it, as fast as they want it, they blame I.T., even when the problem is caused by their personal mobile device, their cell connection, or an app they just downloaded.

Without ecosystem visibility, the curator ends up with unexpected performance problems and unexplained downtime, expensive troubleshooting, and ultimately job loss. No wonder they won't touch shadow I.T.

Visibility brings *flexibility* because the curator can manage the data no matter where it exists. Ultimately this combination brings *job security* to a career that's under attack.

Without these factors in place, you've got surprise upheaval potential in play.

Data Creators

Data creators are all the people who collect and generate data as part of their job.

In corporations, finance, sales, marketing, R&D, and manufacturing all generate mission critical data. In government, these people collect census data, economic information, and intelligence. These are also the people who make movies, design games, and record music for consumers. When creators can't generate data, they're not working.

Do they care about how their data is curated?

No! They couldn't care less.

When I.T. drags their feet, there's a direct impact on the creator's efficiency, effectiveness, and their career.

> DATA CREATORS DON'T CARE HOW THEIR WORK GETS CURATED,
> JUST THAT THEY CAN WORK FAST
> AND THAT IT WON'T GET LOST.

Data creators willingly buy XaaS if necessary to make work possible, easy, and fast. All it takes is a corporate credit card, an easily expensable monthly charge, and they're in business in minutes. Compare this to the usual multi-month response of I.T. This is why business tools providers like Intuit's QuickBooks®, Salesforce.com®, Adobe®, and HubSpot® have grown to be massive companies.

What Data Creators Want

Data creators demand easy *accessibility* to data and *collaboration* systems and choose specialized tools to perform their work with *efficiency*. The result is increased *productivity* and *innovation*. When frustrated, they leave, so *job satisfaction* is key to retaining the best data creators. See Figure 10.

Data Value	Role	Requirements	Result
	Data Consumer		
	Data Creator	Accessibility Collaboration Efficiency	Productivity Innovation Job Satisfaction
	Data Curator		

Figure 10: Nimbility Data Value Hierarchy Data Creator Strategy — Create Data as Efficiently and Innovatively as Possible

The data creators have a pretty good idea about data growth expectations and future requirements that the data curators don't have. When your team designs custom infrastructure, ignoring the creators means you'll underestimate future capacity demand.

Data Creator Business and Nimbility Risk

Data creators often don't consider data protection and business continuity issues. They probably aren't aware of security policy implications and implementations. They may not recognize the business risk of data leakage or compromise. If their favorite XaaS vendor goes down in flames, they're toast.

These all could trigger surprise upheavals.

Data Consumers

Data consumers – at the top of the Nimbility Data Value Hierarchy – rely on data to make executive decisions, formulate battlefield orders, or in the case of consumers, to be entertained or educated. At this level, data becomes mission critical. Easy, secure access to the freshest data becomes a competitive advantage.

Data consumers decide how to spend money to get the data they demand. They are the source of all I.T. (or consumer technology) budgets and they'll invest what they need to accomplish their mission, whether corporate or personal.

What Data Consumers Want

Data consumers expect data to be *reliable, predictable,* and *secure* so they can have *accurate foresight* to direct resources to monetize their data for *profitability* or *mission accomplished.* Or just be entertained or educated. See Figure 11.

Data Value	Role	Requirements	Result
	Data Consumer	Reliability Predictability Security	Accurate Foresight Mission Accomplished Profitability
	Data Creator		
	Data Curator		

Figure 11: Nimbility Data Value Hierarchy Data Creator Strategy — Gain Accurate Foresight to Profitably Monetize Data or Accomplish Their Mission

Data Consumer Business and Nimbility Risk

When data consumers believe that data are accurate, timely, and relevant, they'll make decisions based on reports filtered through their experience, intuition, business model, and objectives. Stale data, inaccurate data, or false data have serious impact on their performance.

For data consumers, data velocity becomes important and decision risk becomes real. Most I.T. innovations target data consumers, such as flash storage provides substantially faster access to data and speeds data mining operations, yet I.T resists these – perceived as risky – innovations.

Watch these factors to prevent surprise upheaval.

The Nimbility Sales Strategy

Let's look at sales, the lifeblood of all organizations. When your team has a limited perspective on sales, you're ripe for upheaval. Let's offer you an upleveled view of sales.

Three factors determine successfully selling to a prospect: 50 percent of your success is based on customer *motivation*, 40 percent is based on your *relationship*, and 10 percent is based on the *product* or service that you're selling.[18] See Figure 12.

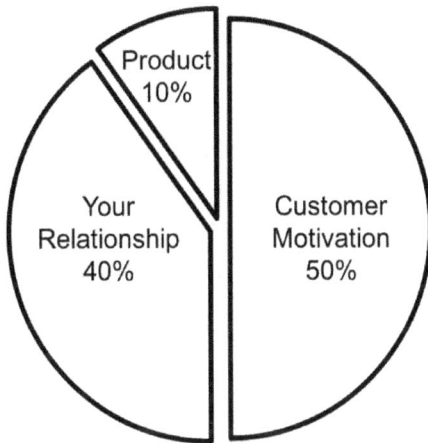

Figure 12: Selling Success Factors

What Happens When There's No Motivation

Half of your success is based on customer *motivation*. Do they want what your product does? Do they have the capacity to consider it right now? Do they find it valuable, relevant, and meaningful? It matters not how good your offer, how great your price, how incredible the deal;

---

[18] This model is adapted from the work of Bruce Joyce about adult learning, which is the essence of selling and change management.

if your prospect isn't motivated, they'll refuse even if you offer to give it to them.

Have you ever experienced the situation where you gave your customer a trial loaner, and when you came back later, they hadn't touched it? No motivation.

> "TO ACT IS TO BE COMMITTED,
> AND TO BE COMMITTED IS TO BE IN DANGER."
> – JAMES BALDWIN

Here's the problem with this tactic: buyers will invent a reason for not paying attention to your product. And their reason isn't good for your position, your brand, or your opportunity for future sales.

Only proceed with sales activity when you understand your customer's motivation or you run the risk of making things worse.

Relationship Powers Sales

The *relationship* with your customer determines if your product is a safe decision. Does your customer trust you? Do they believe you? Do they feel that you're acting in their best interest? Or do they believe you are just trying to manipulate them into buying something that you're spiffed on this week?

> A CUSTOMER BUYS WHEN THEY BECOME CONFIDENT
> ABOUT CHOOSING YOU.

A customer buys when they feel *confident* that you can be trusted, that your product will deliver their desired outcome, and that if there are problems, you'll fix them.

It doesn't matter how motivated the customer; if they don't trust you, they'll choose another, safer place to purchase, except in a dire emergency.

The Secret Sales Accelerator

If you want to really accelerate your sales, map your customer's role temperament, described in the companion book, *The Nimble C-Suite*, so you know exactly how to market to them, communicate with them, motivate, and persuade them, and completely align with their needs and KPIs. You become authentically and non-manipulatively compelling because you will speak their language and know how they make decisions, speeding trust and rapidly building relationship. The competition won't have a chance and will never figure out what hit them; you become their upheaval.[19]

> A TRUSTING CUSTOMER RELATIONSHIP IS THE PRICE
> OF EARNING THE RIGHT TO SELL TO THEM.

Your initial goal is to initiate a relationship that becomes the basis for their confidence. All sales success follows from this.

---

[19] We provide integrity-based sales training and coaching centered on how your customers consider risk and make decisions, shortening the sales cycle. If this might be valuable, let's talk.

Product Positioning When the Time's Right

Surprised that *product* is only 10 percent of your success? You shouldn't be. All of your competitors do a good enough job or no one would buy from them and risk their career. To bash your competition is to insult all those customers who consciously chose them; don't call your customers stupid. Normal psychology states that a person tends to make the best choice based on the information available when they choose. When they selected a competitive product, it was the best choice in that moment.

> INSTEAD OF ASKING, "HOW CAN I BEAT MY COMPETITION?" ASK
> "HOW CAN I HELP MY CUSTOMERS BEAT THEIR COMPETITION?"

Most salespeople put all their attention on the product during a customer conversation.

Big mistake!

That's like going to a doctor's office and the doctor greets you with prescription pad in hand, writing out a drug order.

"Here's what you need" she says, tearing off the 'script.

"Wait a minute, Doc. You don't even know what's wrong with me."

"Sure I do! You're middle age. I know exactly what you need."

"What? What are you talking about?"

"Statins. No doubt you have high cholesterol. Besides, that's what I'm spiffed on this week."

You're laughing because it's true.

"In sales, as in medicine, prescription before diagnosis is malpractice," as *Acorn Principle* author, Jim Cathcart likes to say.

> THE SECRET TO SALES: LEAD WITH THE PROSPECT'S NEED.

Leading with your product creates sales resistance and makes your job so much more challenging.

The Heart of Selling is the 90 Percent

The heart of selling is the 90 percent sum of motivation and relationship. When you can create a trusted relationship and understand your customer's motivation, you can sell them anything that accomplishes their desired outcome. See Figure 13.

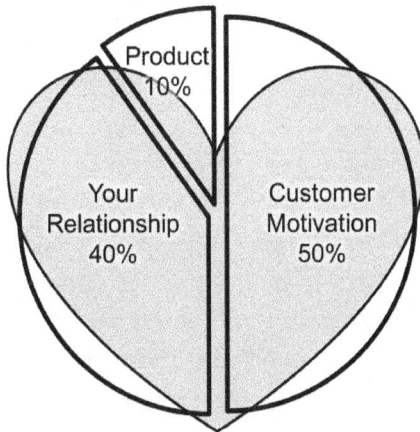

Figure 13: The Heart of Selling is the 90 Percent Combination of Relationship and Motivation

To illustrate this, your team has no doubt successfully sold products that compete with the products they now sell. And they'll probably successfully sell competing products in the future. It's not the product that makes your success, it's their mastery of the 90 percent combination of motivation and relationship. The real competitive difference is your team!

One more proof point: think back to the last time you had a sales challenge. What was the problem? Was it customer motivation, your relationship, or the product? We'll bet it was an unmotivated customer or you didn't clearly understand their motivation.

See how you can use this model to troubleshoot sales problems to become more nimble?

The Nimbility Profit Model for Consistent Results

Every nimble executive focuses on optimizing profits because it rewards the company for the risk, effort, and foresight of running a business and it ensures the company's future.

Our clients always ask us about ways to increase their profits consistently and predictably. Of course, the first actions are to expand value, raise prices, reduce discounts, focus on profitable segments, and cut production costs. This is Business 101, all easier said than done.

Here's a simple, yet elegant model to help predict and capture more profits. See Figure 14.

Figure 14: The Nimbility Profit Model — Consistent Profits Result from Products That are Scarce, Desirable, and Necessary

Consistent profits come from providing your target market with products that are *scarce, desirable,* and *necessary*. Keep in mind that different market segments consider these elements differently. For example, gold may be necessary for manufacturers, desirable for consumers, and scarce for investors.

Scarce

If what you offer is *scarce,* exclusive, unique, or rare then you can set prices that reflect the market demand. Compare this with abundant availability when the price gets set by the lowest-cost producer or the most desperate vendor.

For example, DeBeers® control of the diamond supply inflated prices until Russian-sourced diamonds disrupted the consumer market and now cheap Chinese manufactured diamonds rival the best natural stones.

Marketeers frequently use false scarcity to drive demand, such as using a deadline, expiration date, or limiting quantities. We strongly advise against this tactic, because once a customer is on to you, you'll bust the trust.

Scarcity depends on supply/demand, technology, politics, and culture.

Necessary

When the market *needs* what you offer, they'll get it, or find a substitute for it. This includes items like housing, food, fuel, and utilities.

Necessity depends on culture, geography, and the market.

Desirable

When the market *wants* what you've got, they'll prioritize, pursue, and pay for it. If it's not desirable, you may not be able to give it away. You can increase desirability through marketing.

Over time, what's desirable becomes necessary, described as the Kano Model.[20] A good example: smart phones, which when introduced were desirable and now considered necessary.

Desirability depends on culture, market preferences, perceived scarcity, prestige, and fashion.

When your products miss any of these three elements, profits become unpredictable and variable. Let's dig into these combinations.

---

[20] en.wikipedia.org/wiki/Kano_model

Scarce & Desirable

If your offering is scarce and desirable but not necessary (such as jewelry for consumers), you're offering a *luxury* that provides profit based on market conditions and market discretionary income. You'll do well in up markets and may suffer in down markets.

Add necessity by marketing to target markets that find your offering necessary or prestigious.

Scarce & Necessary

If your offering is scarce and necessary, but not overtly desirable (like *essential* utilities), you've either got a saturated market with little room to improve profits or the market will have well-funded competition (such as solar power versus other ways to generate power). This can be a viable segment for big business, but not for small business.

Add desirability through innovation and marketing.

Necessary & Desirable

If your offering is necessary and desirable but not scarce, you've got a *commodity* where the main differentiation becomes price. Making consistent profits becomes a challenge in a price-driven market.

Add scarcity through innovation, packaging, location, services, marketing, etc.

Predicting Profit Potential

Here's the profit prediction secret to this model: determine whether any of these three factors are increasing or decreasing. You want to choose offerings where the factors are stable or increasing. Decreasing factors indicate a need to upgrade the product, marketing, and target customer, or that you might need to pivot away from this market. This is a sure way to identify potential upheavals.

Put This into Action

❑ Thinking about your main offering, on a scale of 1 to 10 (10 being high), how does your target market think about the scarcity, necessity, and desirability?

❑ What can be improved?

❑ Where are you at risk from competition or changes in culture?

❑ Where could you use some insight about what to do next?

The Nimbility Business Pillars

Business expertise isn't easy, but it is simple. While we fully expect for you to know the content in this next section, we must include it for completeness and for you to use as a review and refinement of your perspective of business essentials.

We've identified seven critical business pillars that uphold a sustainable, scalable, profitable, and salable business. They define the seven key areas of business acumen. When you understand the strategies for each pillar and how to measure success in each area, you can delegate responsibility to direct a complex organization without having to do everything yourself, or worse, perform poorly in a number of the pillars.

We see problems in a business when an executive abdicates responsibility for any of these pillars to someone without understanding of the KPIs, knowing what questions to ask to understand desired outcomes, or lacking the skills to provide strategic direction. More about KPIs on page 122.

> A SEASONED EXECUTIVE WILL NEVER AGREE TO A PROJECT THAT THEY DON'T KNOW HOW TO MANAGE.

While it's appropriate and sane to delegate sequence and tactics, the executive must be responsible for setting strategy and managing to KPIs, timelines, and milestones.

Let's now consider in detail these seven fundamental aspects of every business.

1. Products That Create Unique Value for the Target Market

The product is anything that the organization produces, services they deliver, or environment that they organize.

Every business must have a clearly defined market that identifies with them and their products.

> WHEN YOUR PRODUCT IS FOR EVERYBODY, YOU'LL FIND YOU'RE SELLING TO NOBODY.

The key take-away: organizations must target customers who identify with what they sell. You do this by aligning with customer values, tuning the product message directly to them by speaking their language, providing unique value, selling the way that they want to buy, and delivering their desired outcomes.

Customers select products that reflect their personal identity. Never has this been truer than today, illustrated by the vast product portfolios available from many different manufacturers.

This concept of identity also comes into play for government and education organizations. City and state governments choose business rules – tax incentives, mandates, technology, environment, and outreach – to encourage certain types of citizens and businesses to choose their locations. This is how they define community culture, their product.

> CUSTOMERS BUY TO SUPPORT AND UP-LEVEL THEIR SELF-IDENTITY.

For example, Nevada has for decades enjoyed a booming economy by offering a relaxed stance on gambling and other vices. When other states offered lottery and other gaming opportunities, Nevada refined their product by pivoting their business model to entertainment, meetings, and world-class restaurants. "What happens in Vegas, stays in Vegas" creates a liberal environment that lures conventioneers and vacationers. Little do most visitors realize that this slogan actually refers to gambling money, as tourists substantially understate how much they've lost and overstate how much they've won. People come to Las Vegas to have outrageous experiences that aren't available elsewhere so they can bring home bragging rights.

Being a viable organization means understanding your customer's customer better than anyone else. Yes, this means someone on your team must do this research because customers often can't do objective research on their own. One powerful way to do this is with Customer Advisory Boards, where you collaborate with customer executives on your joint future.

KPIs of product success include market penetration, speed of market adoption, level of competitive disruption, maintaining product margin over time, gross margin against market average, etc.

Virtually every business demands a well thought out product development plan because this is fundamental to effective business model pivots and upheaval avoidance.

2. Marketing That Triggers Relevant Conversations

Marketing is everything that you do *before* you have a meaningful customer conversation. It takes them on the journey from being unaware to aware, to interested, to asking for a conversation, whether that's in person or via your web presence.

If your marketing doesn't trigger a relevant conversation, it's not marketing, it's a waste of money.

> WHEN YOU HAVE TO COLD CALL TO FIND CUSTOMERS,
> YOUR MARKETING IS BROKEN.

Relevance is the key. We can get you conversations all day long: "$100 gift card when you book an appointment!" All that happens is you waste time and money trying to persuade a non-decision maker into introducing you to their boss. Not going to happen.

The best marketing provides prospects with outcome-based education, focusing on the benefit of the results. It teaches customers how to buy what you sell.

One of the best books on marketing is *Guerrilla Marketing* by Mark's co-author, the late, great Jay Conrad Levinson. Focusing on what works, Jay's words of wisdom are still worth studying and implementing.

Every sustainable, scalable business has a formal marketing plan. These plans demand I.T. to implement, track, mine, and manage prospect data, which is why marketing buys more I.T. than the data center.

YOU REAP IN SALES WHAT YOU SOW IN MARKETING.

Marketing KPIs include the number of conversations generated, the quality of the conversation (are those inquiring qualified), and the sales cycle time (where are customers in their purchase journey when they ask for a conversation), projected future sales pipeline, and average forecast deal size.

3. Sales That Facilitates Mutually Profitable Transactions

Sales is the customer-centered conversations that fill in the information gaps, organize the details, eliminate customer concerns, and make sure that you are the only desirable, safe choice.

As you've learned earlier in this chapter, only ten percent of sales success rests on the products or services. The rest is based on mapping customer motivation to the offering and building a trusted relationship.

The reason we use the word *facilitate* is because the notion of *closing* sales is false and narcissistic. There is only facilitation unless you have signature authority on your customer's bank account.

We've only known one salesman who had that power. Gary was the top salesman in a regional lumber yard chain, outselling the number two salesman by a factor of three. His secret: he actively managed his customers' construction projects with his goal to keep the crew on site, building, not running to the store for supplies and tools, resulting in a typical completion date six weeks sooner than the industry average. In exchange, he insisted on being paid daily for what was delivered and used on the jobsite. He had signature authority on a desk drawer full of customer checkbooks. That's a trusted partner!

> THE DEAL CLOSES WHEN THE CUSTOMER'S READY AND NOT UNTIL.

Deals must be *mutually profitable* or someone is getting robbed and the relationship isn't sustainable. Your best customers want you to be successful. They want you to stay in business because you are an important part of their business model. While they don't want to be gouged, they're willing to pay you a fair profit and expect you to cover your expenses on every deal.

> NO DEADLINE, NO DEAL.

Part of the responsibility of sales is *forecasting*. This allows the rest of operations to get a handle on demand and assign resources to deliver. There's a difference between a pipeline and a forecast. A *pipeline* consists of prospects who have made a decision your way and are moving toward making a commitment, the purchase order. A forecast tracks customer with an internal deadline, but no decision. If the customer doesn't have a deadline, it's not a deal, it's a wish. When working with high ticket sales, accurate forecasts become more important because of the magnitude of resources required to deliver the customer purchase on time.

Every sustainable, scalable, profitable, and salable business has a formal sales strategy, complete with a well-defined culture, formal sales methodology, sales playbook, consistent sales training, sales management systems, and on-going sales reviews. And they routinely reposition the lowest sales performer to a better fit for their skills.

Sales KPIs include deal size, forecast accuracy, and sales and operating margins.

4. Service That Earns Customer Loyalty

Until your customer experiences you, there is no loyalty. When customers consider that they got what they paid for and nothing more, there is no loyalty, it was a fair exchange. They owe you nothing more.

It's when customers feel that they got more than they paid for, usually in meaning, insight, and foresight, that they feel like they hit the jackpot.

> UNTIL YOU DELIVER BEYOND WHAT A CUSTOMER EXPECTS
> AND PAYS FOR, THERE IS NO LOYALTY.

Customer service is the investment that you make in the *next* sale. You might consider it to be marketing to existing customers, a worthwhile investment because you'll make more money on the second transaction than you will the first.

Here's why, since the customers must manage the perception of risk in high consideration purchases, your customers will likely first make a small purchase, preferring to have a phased deployment to manage and mitigate risk. Always be earning the right to sell the next phase of the deployment.

Customer service drives the most desirable of marketing activity, referrals. Yet, referrals are earned. Teach and motivate your customer service people to harvest referrals and they'll become one of the most profitable parts of your customer acquisition system.

Service KPIs include percentage of customers that repeat purchase, customer satisfaction scores, and the number of referrals generated.

5. Operations That Scale with Economic Cycles

We've recently gone through an era where businesses crashed and burned because of an economic downturn. Many failed because they couldn't downsize fast enough. This is a case where efficiency failed and flexibility had real value.

> YOU CAN THRIVE IN BUSINESS DURING GOOD TIMES AND BAD IF YOU CAN FLEXIBLY SCALE WITH VARYING DEMAND.

Customers willingly pay slightly more for flexibility, including the ability to change how much they consume, what they consume, and when they consume it.

Savvy execs attempt to outsource as much of their production as they can, converting much of their fixed capital costs to variable operating expense. Yet this comes with the demand that you partner with vendors who can scale along with your operation and align with your culture and values.

Operations KPIs reflect the ability to make rapid changes and efficiency of the processes.

6. Finance That Controls Cash Flow and Funds the Future

Cash flow is king, as the old business mantra goes. Without solid cash flow and working capital management system in place, including tying sales expenses to product cost, a business operates with a risky business model.

This includes government and education organizations because they have to match cash outflow with tax and tuition revenue inflows. If they can't, they must borrow money bringing a whole new set of complexities, because the source of funds determines the business model.

> CASH FLOW IS KING. IF YOU WANT FULL CONTROL OF YOUR DESTINY, YOU'VE GOT TO SELF-FUND YOUR BUSINESS.

By embracing a primarily operating expense (OpEx) model, business can retain more earnings to fund growth, such as investing in new products, marketing, and sales.

A common long-term business challenge is declining margins over time as companies cut pricing in an attempt to compete with new market entrants. Many a successful company has crashed and burned when margins eroded and replacement products weren't ready. Helping your team integrate product development with cash flow and funding management can substantially increase the probably of long-term success.

Financial KPIs include cash flow levels, cash flow velocity, and operating capital levels and trends.

7. Culture That Upholds a Unique Brand Experience

Many companies underestimate the power of culture. Culture is the unspoken or codified business rules of conduct that define how the company team behaves, how they treat each other, and ultimately how they treat customers. Culture determines the success of the chosen business model.

> CULTURE DETERMINES HOW WE TREAT EACH OTHER:
> EMPLOYEES, PROSPECTS, CUSTOMERS, AND THE PLANET.

Culture overrules everything, whether it's defined, allowed, or tolerated. No matter what the mission statement or business rules, culture dominates the tone of business.

Most entrepreneurial businesses start out with the founder's personal culture being the company culture. As the company grows, the founder hires people they know and so easily align with that undocumented culture.

When the company grows beyond the founder's family and friends, they inadvertently hire people who don't share their same culture and the company starts to deviate as these new people begin to hire and manage to their personal culture.

The only way to keep this from happening is to define culture and have it reflected in the business model and business rules. Culture ultimately defines the company's *brand*. Some still operate under a false assumption that culture is organic; that it can't be created. That's allowing the tail to wag the dog. Culture architecture is a fine art that can be mastered with the right mentors.

KPIs for culture can include customer satisfaction scores (yes, this is where this belongs), customer alignment with stated target customer goals, employee satisfaction scores (there are very specific dimensions to have them rate), and personal satisfaction of the executive team.

What is Nimbility Branding?

Let's explore the concept of brand for a moment. Branding is more than a logo, color palate, or any other design element. Branding is the customer's expectation of a certain experience.

> BRANDING MAKES THE PROMISE OF A CERTAIN CUSTOMER EXPERIENCE, THEREFORE REDUCING PURCHASE RISK.

The history of branding goes back to the days when cattle ran free in the open range of the United States. Cattle owners marked their herd with a hot branding iron. When the cowboys drove the livestock to market, buyers over time could identify which cattle had better pasture, better care, better water and therefore would taste superior. They would say, "I want that brand."

Nimbility Branding is:
1. A customer *experience* that
2. They *value*
3. They willingly *pay* for

4. They want to *repeat*
5. Not *available* elsewhere
6. They'll *tell* others about.

If any of these six elements is missing, it's not a sustainable, scalable, nor nimble brand. Brand experience happens at every touch point a customer has with the company environment, products, and people.

Brand gets reinforced through the design of I.T. systems, ensuring that the team delivers the desired customer experience and offers ways of managing exceptions that indicate a potential business rule change. Systems with too much rigidity open them to competition that can better respond to customer expectations and demands with reduced friction.

How All This Fits Together

Identify the business pillars that you and your team need to master. It can be as easy as reading a book, taking a course, or hiring a business coach or consultant to fill in the blanks, identify your blind spots, and develop KPIs to monitor, manage, and improve your business. Yes, we can help.

When working with your customer, have conversations about their business pillars and how they measure and manage success with their KPIs. Look at how they implement the KPIs as business rules into their systems. Support the success of their KPIs and they become loyal, and you'll intercept upheavals. This is how you help them beat their competition.

Consider offering your customers ideas on how to improve the KPIs with better business models and better culture, resulting in a sustainable, scalable, profitable, and ultimately salable business, becoming a valued business partner.

Go ahead, buy them a copy of this book.

Chapter Summary

❑ Having a clear, concise picture of business elements increases Nimbility.

❑ Understanding the elements of the Nimbility Business Model Cycle helps identify potential sources of upheavals.

❑ The source of funds determines a company's business model. Changes in funding sources drive changes in the business model, often triggering avoidable upheavals.

❑ Artificial Intelligence can inadvertently trigger upheavals unless it's properly trained and overseen.

❑ Key Performance Indicators (KPIs) increase Nimbility when properly selected and used. Choose a mix of leading, current, and lagging indicators depending on if the person measured is strategic or tactical.

❑ Poorly selected KPIs can trigger unnecessary and avoidable upheavals.

❑ Data is the lifeblood of business. The Nimbility Data Value Hierarchy allows you to better understand how your team considers and values data so that you can become more nimble with the data.

❑ The Nimbility Sales Strategy puts in right sequence the three factors of sales success: customer motivation, relationship, and product. This simplifies the sales process and enables rapid troubleshooting.

❑ The Nimbility Profit Model allows you to predict and prevent profit upheavals by identifying market changes that require attention. It also allows you to profitability design product.

❑ The Nimbility Business Pillars:
1. Products that create unique value for the target market
2. Marketing that triggers relevant conversations
3. Sales that facilitate mutually profitable transactions
4. Service that earns customer loyalty
5. Operations that scale with economic cycles
6. Finance that controls cash flow and funds the future
7. Culture that upholds a unique brand experience

❑ Nimbility Branding is:
1. A customer experience that
2. They value
3. They willingly pay for
4. They want to repeat
5. Not available elsewhere
6. They'll tell others about.

Ask Yourself

❑ How well do I and my team really understand key business elements? Is this gap potentially an opening for upheavals?

❑ How does our source of funds impact our business model and culture? Is this a potential for avoidable upheavals?

❑ How meaningful to me are my team's KPIs? Do I get the right leading, current, and lagging data I need to confidently lead? Does my team have any KPIs that might be misleading or misdirecting?

- ❑ Where may I have misalignment of my team in the Nimbility Data Value Hierarchy?
- ❑ How can the Nimbility Sales Strategy help me sharpen our sales methods?
- ❑ How do our products stack up with the Nimbility Profit Model? Are there signs of an impending profit upheaval? What can I do right now to prevent this?
- ❑ How comfortable am I with each of the Nimbility Business Pillars? Where might there be understanding gaps that make me blind to potential upheavals? How can I fill those gaps?
- ❑ How many of the Nimbility branding factors do we have in play? What can I do to make our brand more nimble to prevent upheavals?

Ask Your Team

- ❑ How well do you understand our business model? If we could uplevel your understanding, how might that help you with your role?
- ❑ What are your key performance indicators? Do you feel you have full control over them? Do you think that they are meaningful in how they measure your performance? What do we need to consider changing to bring them into alignment with your role?
- ❑ Do you consider yourself a data curator, a data creator, or a data consumer? How can we help you better work with data to support your role?
- ❑ How well do you understand sales? What might be the value of upleveled sales skills?
- ❑ Where do you think we could improve our profitability? What factors should we consider when doing this? How could we predict future profitability?

❏ How well do you understand the elements of our business? If we upleveled that understanding, how do you think that would benefit your role?

❏ What do you think *brand* means? How can we increase the value of our brand?

Action Plan

❏ Review your business model against the Nimbility Business Model Cycle, looking for understanding gaps. Fill those gaps.

❏ Consider how AI can be used to reduce upheavals.

❏ Review your team's KPIs for relevance, suitability, and meaningfulness to their role, and how they allow you to better lead and direct them. Fix any KPI that isn't suitable.

❏ Review your team's relationship with data in light of the Nimbility Data Value Hierarchy. Where do you need to adjust to prevent upheavals?

❏ Think about your sales processes in light of the Nimbility Sales Strategy. How can you shorten your sales cycle and increase profits by applying this model?

❏ Examine your products through the lens of the Nimbility Profit Model. Where are you missing profit opportunities? Where can you detect potential profit upheavals that can be addressed now?

❏ Review the Nimbility Business Pillars for understanding gaps. Fill those gaps.

❏ Review your branding strategy in the light of the Nimbility Branding Strategy. Where can you add value to your branding that will prevent upheavals?

Chapter 6:
Upgrades Required to Deploy a Nimble Company

Before you can deploy a nimble company, you'll need to make sure your team possesses key Nimbility skills with systems in place to let them use those skills to the greatest effect. Without these skills or systems, it will be difficult to form and lead a nimble company.[21]

Upgrade Your Team

Your team most likely requires upleveling of their personal Nimbility skills, those elements that bring them consistent Nimbility. There are three key Nimbility components:

❑ Mindset – how your team thinks, the temperament lens they use to view their world, and the mental resources they use make decisions

❑ Skillset – your team's ability to perform strategic and tactical tasks to optimally fulfill their role and responsibility

---

[21] Parts of this chapter are also found in the companion book, *The Nimble C-Suite*. We include it here for completeness. For the full executive discussion, see the companion book.

{ 163 }

❑ Toolset – the models, policies, software, reports, systems, processes, and procedures that enable your team to efficiently deliver their required results.

Complete this upleveling with mentoring and coaching that ensures skills integration into daily routines.

Uplevel to a Nimble Mindset

Let's take a closer look at team mindset as defined by their perspective lens. Our worldview is set by our experiences, training, culture, personal norms, religious or spiritual practices, and mental health.

For example, a narcissist has a warped lens about their personal importance, while one who is arrogant resists other viewpoints because they are afraid of losing status when they are proven wrong. A sociopath doesn't care about the wellbeing of others and insists that the end justifies the means – a viewpoint that enlightened consumers consider repugnant, especially for a socially responsible company.

Promote a Fluid Perspective Lens

Being nimble requires intentional fluidity with your perspective lens because a rigid lens has blind spots. Understanding the lenses of your team brings their perspective into sharp focus that enables you to tap into their diverse perspectives to extract a broader range of wisdom than you can access on your own. While each role demands a specific lens for daily operations, the ability to envision through other lenses brings powerful understanding, and access to new unrealized resources.

Encourage your team to regularly take on their peers' perspectives as part of the decision-making process.

While this may be a challenge for some, if this level of maturity is beyond a particular executive or manager to do, that person doesn't belong in leadership. Yes, it will be easier for those who have had true debate training, where arguing the opposite side of the issue is de rigueur. This brings a broad-perspective mindset to all key team members, which results in the ability to consider options that may have previously been unthinkable.

Once your team experiences lens fluidity, they become open to upleveling their skills

Key Skills Training for Collaboration Nimbility

This book has guided you through the many elements to consider, both strategically and tactically, when building a nimble company. You probably have identified areas where your culture and your team need upgrades.

Key areas to consider:

❑ Identity development – Does everyone on your team have a self-concept that supports their role and responsibility? Do they see themselves as nimble, confident, humble, resilient, innovative? Does their behavior reflect their necessary identity? What unresourceful identity elements do they need to outgrow, such as overreliance on a specific leadership style?

❑ Mindset development – Mindset follows identity. Mindset is also impacted by corporate and personal culture, assigned KPIs, and the lens on their role and responsibility. Does each team member's mindset completely support their role and responsibility?

❑ Skillset development – Do all of your team members have the leadership, communications, negotiating, decision-making, analytics, and technical skills required for their role?

❑ Toolset development – What tools do each of your team members need to build or master to deliver peak performance? Do any of them resist using new tools?

❑ Skills integration – Do you have team members who need mentoring or coaching to consistently integrate their skills into daily activities? Do they need an accountability partner to keep them on their growing edge and prevent them from reverting to old, unresourceful behaviors? Identify who does and see that they are paired with the right partner.

The fastest path is with outside, professional help. Identify who can diagnose and prescribe upgrades for individuals on your team, and for your team as a whole. This investment will pay dividends for a lifetime.

The Plan for Team Changes with Succession and Grooming

Team upheavals are inevitable and shouldn't be a complete surprise. People retire, choose a different life or career path, have family needs that drive job changes, experience extended illness, and occasionally unexpectedly pass away.

The upheavals literate executive makes plans for promotions and succession, knowing that this is a necessary part of their routine strategy development. This includes ongoing training through the Chief Integrity Officer in corporate culture development, skill building, and perspective expansion. It means creating a corporate culture of learning, including personal and professional growth.

We discuss this in depth in the companion book, *The Nimble C-Suite.*

The best nimble teams grow from within because they know that bringing in outside executives who are upheaval illiterate can slow them down or derail them entirely.

New Nimble Attitudes

Consider this list of nimble attitudes as you lead forward your nimble team.

Be Soft on People, Hard on Tasks

The Harvard Negotiation Study found that the most effective outcomes came when leadership was soft on people (compassionate) and hard on tasks (accountability).

> PROMOTING SELF-ESTEEM WITHOUT ANCHORING IT IN ACTUAL ACCOMPLISHMENTS, SIMPLY ENDS UP INCREASING NARCISSISM.
> – KEN WILBER

Soft on people doesn't mean indulging a poor performer but seeing that despite having the best intentions they have insufficient training, an incomplete perspective, or personal issues, that cause a gap between their intentions and their behaviors.

Balance Transformation with Stability

Do so without the expense of one or the other, because transformation without stability breeds chaos, and stability without transformation breeds stagnancy and status quo addiction.

Clearly Understand and Effectively Implement Principles, Policies, and Procedures

Principles, Policies, and Procedures connect strategy to tactical implementation, so an organization walks its talk.

Principles are the universal guidelines that support a nimble organization. Every team member requires training in your core principles and how to correctly use them. Guiding principles for decision-making provide a framework that equips your people to make wise choices within their scope of authority and responsibility.

A *policy* is a set of guidelines that outline the organization's plan for tackling various issues. An effective policy outlines what employees must do or not do, and directions, limits, and guidance for decision making. Policies are set by the executive team, with sub-policies set by the management team. Becoming policy-heavy kills motivation, engagement, and culture. Reserve policies for hard limits on behaviors with legal ramifications, such as physical and data security policies.

A *procedure* explains a specific, detailed tactical action plan for carrying out a principle or policy. It shows employees the who, how, and when to deal with a situation, step-by-step.

Upgrade Your Communication and Collaboration Processes for Nimbility

Let's discuss what to upgrade in your approach to communication and team collaboration.

Employee Review and Upgrade Procedures

Conventional employee review processes tend to kill nimbility, destroy culture, severely limit innovation, and hobble performance. They occur too infrequently (most commonly annually) and they typically focus on whether someone gets a raise, a promotion, or is fired.

While those are important decisions, the primary purpose of performance reviews in nimble companies is personnel growth. Growth doesn't happen once a year. It unfolds continuously. This means that support and modification must occur regularly. That might mean every quarter, every couple of weeks, or something in between. A person's role, newness to the role, and temperament determine how often these reviews need to occur.

Accountability-Capable Agreements Procedure

Four integrated accountability procedures ensure continuous executive, employee, and team development. They are:

❑ Accountability-Capable Agreements
❑ Best Practices Upgrades
❑ Implementation Breakdown Repairs
❑ Performance Reviews that include Collaborative Disengagement when appropriate.

In today's world, good intentions are substitutes for agreements or get treated as though they are agreements. This sets the stage for unnecessary conflict. When a good intention is a substitute for a commitment, nothing gets done even though everyone means well. When a good intention is treated like an agreement, everyone has a different idea about what the commitment entails, which leads to disappointments and a potential chain reaction of missed handoffs and deadlines. This causes unnecessary upheavals.

Accountability-Capable Agreements

An *accountability-capable agreement* procedure specifies three things: observables, attributes, and time frames.

❑ *Observables* are what an independent witness would see did or didn't occur.

❑ *Attributes* are specifications about what resources are needed to get the task done and what constitutes excellence.

❑ *Time frames* are determined after looking at sequencing: what needs to be done by whom, in what order, how long each step should realistically take, and who gets each handoff.

Agreements also include a commitment to provide immediate updates if complications arise that result in needing to revise the time frame or resources needing to be utilized.

All agreements are in writing to prevent misunderstanding about the nature of the agreement. This can be a simple email to all involved that details the three elements discussed above.

Best Practices Upgrade Procedure

Nimble organizations are regularly upgrading their best practices. The procedure for this has two steps: blessing what is going well and "even better ifs."

Blessing what is going well means being very specific about what that is and why it's valuable. The reason for saying why it's valuable is that this embeds training in impact literacy.

People are more likely to do the right thing when they see their positive impacts when they do well, and they see their negative impacts when they don't. Only addressing the negative teaches people to operate from an *avoid* viewpoint instead of the desired *embrace* viewpoint.

"Even better ifs" are a way to enhance Nimbility instead of getting caught in gripe sessions that build bad feelings.

In this second part of the Best Practices Upgrade procedure, people offer brainstorms about how something could be done even better, the superior outcome this would create, and the benefits this outcome would provide.

Once brainstorming is complete, an elevated best practice is selected, and this becomes an additional accountability-capable agreement that is added to each person's accountability-capable agreements list.

Implementation Breakdown Repair

Even when accountability-capable agreements are recorded and best practices upgrades are being implemented, unexpected complications can still occur that cause breakdowns in agreement implementation or collaboration effectiveness.

When these breakdowns occur, they need to be dealt with in ways that lead to improved effectiveness and collaboration instead of lingering conflict and resentment.

The *Implementation Breakdown Repair* procedure is a four-step process for turning breakdowns into engagement, collaboration, and accountability upgrades. These four steps include each person stating:

❑ Their own unintended contributions to the breakdown

❑ The unintended negative impacts their unintended contributions had

❑ The impact repair they will do when a repair is feasible

❑ How they will handle future similar situations more effectively than they knew how to do in the current situation.

That upgrade plan is then recorded as another accountability-capable agreement. (Training is usually required before Breakdown Repair procedures can be fruitfully conducted. We stand ready to provide your team with that training.)

Performance Review Procedure

The performance review session is conducted like a best practices upgrades session, except that the items that are reviewed are that person's or team's accountability-capable agreements, and whatever has been added to that list as a result of best practices upgrades sessions and breakdown repair sessions.

Performance reviews also include another item: *growth edges*. The individual or team selects a top growth edge to focus on between performance reviews. During each review, progress with that growth edge is discussed and a plan for going the next step or selecting a new growth edge is agreed upon. This is revisited during the next performance review. Growth edges are specified using the guidelines for accountability-capable agreements.

Collaborative Disengagement Procedure

Can you see the positive impact of integrating accountability-capable agreements, best practices upgrades, breakdown repair upgrades, and performance reviews that include growth edges?

This approach helps people hold themselves accountable, and this in turn makes it clear when a raise, a promotion, or disengagement is called for.

Collaborative disengagement, as paradoxical as that term might sound, occurs when someone undergoing performance reviews sees a pattern of not completing agreements. This doesn't necessarily mean they are a bad person or even a lazy person. It always means that they are not right matched to the role they fill. Collaborative disengagement is simply an acknowledgment that a wrong match exists between a person and a role. (It should be noted that conducting collaborative disengagement meetings well requires some training and also that these should only occur after consulting with your corporate attorney.)

When collaborative disengagement is necessary and is done well, this can have very positive company and community reputation impacts on online employee review sites such as GlassDoor.com. It can also reduce the chances that an employee will sue for wrongful termination.

Chapter Summary

☐ To deploy a nimble company requires key upgrades including identity, mindset, skillset, toolset, and skills integration.

❑ Key collaboration skills development brings critical capability to innovate and be resilient.
❑ Nimble attitudes keep the team on track.
❑ Critical skills: developing accountability-capable agreements, best practices upgrades, implementation breakdown repairs, and collaborative disengagement procedures.
❑ Upleveling to nimble performance reviews consistently uplevels team performance, instead of demoralizing them as most review processes do.

Ask Yourself

❑ How do I need to uplevel my identity? What old views do I need to drop and what new views do I want to take on?
❑ Where do I need to uplevel my mindset?
❑ Where do I need to uplevel my skillset?
❑ Where do I need to uplevel my toolset?
❑ Could I have blind spots in these four areas? Who can I trust to give me qualified insight?
❑ What could be the value of bringing accountability-capable agreements into my company? What would it cost if I didn't?
❑ What would be the value of bringing into my company the rest of the accountability skills stack (best practices upgrades, implementation breakdown repairs, and collaborative disengagement procedures)? What would it cost if I didn't?
❑ How could the Nimbility performance review procedure consistently improve my team's performance?

Ask Your Team

❏ If you were to uplevel your abilities to become more innovative and resilient, where would you start?

❏ Where do you see us hampered by lack of accountability? What's the impact on our ability to execute?

❏ If we implemented accountability-capable agreements, what do you think would be the impact on your role and on the company generally?

❏ Where do we need to uplevel our ability to collaborate? What would it be worth for us to do this?

Action Plan

❏ Identify where your team must uplevel their mindset, skillset, and toolset for your company to become nimble.

❏ Determine the value of doing this. Determine the cost of not doing this.

❏ Create a plan to do this, starting with your key executives.

❏ Identify where you could use some help in designing and deploying these upgrades.

❏ Measure the impact on execution risk as your team improves collaboration skills and implements accountability-capable agreements.

Chapter 7:
Your Plan to Win

Now it's time to put your plan in action. You've considered the key points in this book. You've argued with yourself and debated your team on key trends, execution risk, and business issues and come to some conclusions.[22] What's next?

Build Your Strategic Map

Create a strategic map of what you want to accomplish and why you want to accomplish it.

Share this strategic map with your executive team and select portions of it to share with your operations team. But keep in mind, as the responsible executive, you set the direction.

> YOUR BUSINESS ISN'T A PURE DEMOCRACY.
> EMPLOYEES DON'T GET TO VOTE ON STRATEGY.

---

[22] Portions of this chapter are also found in the companion book, *The Nimble C-Suite*. They are included here for completeness. For the full, executive focused discussion, see the companion book.

Build Your Action Plan Sequence

Round up all of the action steps you've identified in this book. Choose a deployment timeline with milestones and KPIs. You can't do everything at once, but you can take your next indicated step right now, and the next one when the time is right, and so forth. This is how you'll start the transformation and stay on track. Count on adjusting on the way; there is no one-size-fits-all plan.

Work with Your Team to Deploy

Your team is the execution engine that makes all this work. Guide them with your new direction and challenge them to unlearn and relearn these new business models.

Some of them won't make it. Some of them will embrace this new model. Others might wait and see. Cut loose those who resist so the wait and see group can pivot from reluctant to supportive.

Tactical deployment is an ever-moving target. You need a flexible team to make your business work well.

> SUCCESS IS NOT A MATTER OF LUCK, IT'S A MATTER OF DISCIPLINE.

Once you design, document, and operate your upgraded business model, you'll have a business with recurring revenue that is sustainable, scalable, profitable, ultimately saleable, because it is responsive to a transformation economy in which consumers, employees, executives, and vendors choose businesses that are socially responsible.

Selling Ideas to the Team

When selling your ideas to your team, approach this with the mindset and skillset of an ethical salesperson. Review the elements of sales success (aligning motivation, relationship, and desired change) on page 136 and put them into action.

This means your ideas must have:

- ❏ Mission, vision, and brand integrity alignment
- ❏ Cultural and values alignment
- ❏ Team motivational alignment
- ❏ Team KPI alignment.

> INVOLUNTARY CHANGE IN THE ABSENCE OF AN EXPLORER MINDSET
> IS ALWAYS PAINFUL.

Any changes to the status quo must be shown to improve performance over what the team has already agreed with or you're going to have to reset expectations and prepare for a team upheaval. Change, even when voluntary, can feel painful or evoke fear.

Celebrate Wins, Small and Large

When making changes, celebrating wins maintains motivation because all on the team have opportunities to honor the progress that helps them value positive change. Think of celebrations as blessing rituals. Let your culture determine how to celebrate. Ask your employees how they'd like to celebrate hitting key goals. They'll probably ask for less than you're willing to fund.

Small wins get small celebrations. Employee of the week and the month goes a long way. Shortening decision cycles gets a celebration. A new major customer gets a celebration.

Large wins get large celebrations. Exceeding targets, competitive wins, new product release, and market recognition get bigger celebrations.

How to Troubleshoot Nimbility Issues

Your first step is to determine if you're facing a systems problem or a people problem. If it's a systems problem, do a deep dive into the execution risk factors starting on page 37 to identify the root causes.

When troubleshooting people issues, first solve for mindset, then for skillset, and then for toolset. This sequencing is a prime leadership principle.

Now we'll discuss what you'll need to consider, in the psychologically wise order, and a way to illuminate the root causes of the challenges you'll face.

What is Their Maslow's Hierarchy of Needs Level?

You've almost certainly been exposed to Maslow's Hierarchy of Needs. Even though it was first published by Abraham Maslow in 1943 and has been criticized by some academics, we view it as helpful for quickly troubleshooting mindset problems. See Figure 15.

Self-actualization:
problem solving,
morality, spontaneity,
creativity, lack of
prejudice, accepts facts

Esteem: self-esteem, confidence,
achievement, respect of others,
respects others

Love/Belonging: friendship, family,
sexual intimacy

Safety: security of body, of employment, of resources,
of morality, of the family, of health, of property

Physiological: breathing, water, excretion, sleep, food,
homeostasis, sex

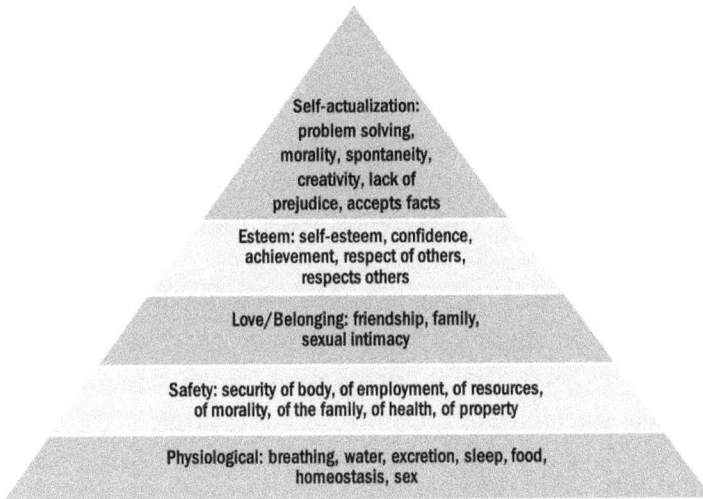

Figure 15: Maslow's Hierarchy of Needs Helps Quickly
Identify What to Address to Guide a Team Member to Peak
Performance

Let's do a quick review of this hierarchy with an eye toward applying it to leadership. Maslow pointed out that our needs on the lower levels of the hierarchy must be substantially met before we can fully access the higher levels.

For example, when a team member is at one of the two lowest levels because of an unmet physiological or psychological need, their ability to access higher cognitive functions will be quite limited. At these lower levels, they primarily pay attention to the immediate needs of their body or their psyche.

Step one is to check in. How are you doing? How are you feeling? How's the family? Is everything alright? If they've just lost their family pet, been served with divorce papers, worried about a sick relative, etc., they must address this before being able to consider another topic.

Help them any way you can and defer any decisions until they've formulated a plan to resolve these personal life challenges so they can restore life balance. Inspiration to do better doesn't become fully useful until one is within the upper three levels.

An important aspect of Maslow's work: if we get frustrated at a higher level, we'll revert to a lower level. This is likely part of the explanation for why solid performers start to underperform when thwarted.

Nimbility Mindset Factors

Next, check in on their mindset factors. The topic of mindset usually centers around a *fixed* mindset or *growth* mindset, as popularized by Carol Dweck's book *Mindset: The New Psychology of Success.*

You're about to take that up a notch so you can bring mindset into nimble territory. See Figure 16.

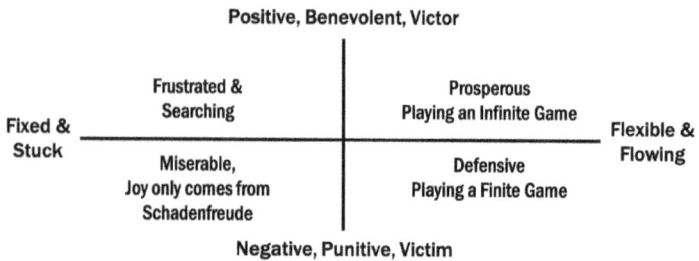

Positive, Benevolent, Victor

	Frustrated & Searching	Prosperous Playing an Infinite Game	
Fixed & Stuck			Flexible & Flowing
	Miserable, Joy only comes from Schadenfreude	Defensive Playing a Finite Game	

Negative, Punitive, Victim

Figure 16: Nimbility Mindset Factors — Expected Outcomes (Horizontal Axis) Versus Worldview Frame (Vertical Axis) Determines Mindset

The figure's horizontal axis is the fixed versus growth mindset spectrum. We define growth as flexible and flowing. Adding the vertical axis of worldview frame and how they expect the ecosystem to impact their plans, creates a map of what's driving mindset.

You can quickly diagnose their mindset by how they respond to your conversations. Are they frustrated and searching? Are they miserable and only finding joy when others are defeated? Are they defensive and expecting winners and losers? Or do they enjoy a prosperity mindset where we all play to play again?

How to Catalyze Rapid Mindset Shifts

Help them navigate to the prosperous nimble quadrant, where one plays an infinite game. Ed Oakley, co-author of *Enlightened Leadership* shares these questions to help rapidly shift mindset: [23]

❏ *What's going well?* Keep following up their answer with, "What else…" until they run out of answers. This shifts them to a positive view of recent history, and of reviewing recent wins.

❏ *Why is it going well?* Follow up with, "What else…" until they run out of answers. This rounds up resources, identifies that the environment supports progress, and shows them how they win.

❏ *What do you want to change?* Don't start with this question because without the prior two questions, it becomes a complaints session instead of a growth session. With the more positive view and resources,

---

[23] Ed generously agreed for us to share this with you.

change doesn't look so daunting. Let them make one suggestion so that it doesn't become overwhelming.

❏ *Why do you want to change this?* This question rounds up the motivation and ultimately the willingness to change.

❏ *What do you see as the path to how we can do this?* This tests to see if they're ready to take the next step and makes them part of the process, a surefire way to garner support for the new destination.

> WHAT WE CREATE WE SUPPORT.
> – DAN CLARK

Use this simple yet powerful way to help them find their way out of a mindset hole that has trapped them.

Is the Problem Don't Know, Can't Do, or Don't Care?

Next, see if the gap is lack of ability, action, or attitude. Ask yourself, is the problem "don't know," "can't do," or "don't care?" Your gut reaction will likely be accurate. It may be that two of these issues are getting in the way at the same time.

The solution to ___ is ___:

❏ Don't know – Train and coach them.

❏ Can't do – Help them identify and access the tools to do the job or redeploy them into a role that fits their capabilities.

❏ Don't care – Check on motivation and fix it, or move them to where they do care, or enact Collaborative Disengagement (see page 173).

This simple tactic works wonders to troubleshoot and fix people problems.

Get Help from Experts

Our company, NimbilityWorks.com, helps companies like yours become a better version of themselves because their customers want to become a better version of themselves. See more on page 199.

We can help you with this transition. We can be your interim Chief Integrity Officer until you have one in place.

Share Your Story

We can't wait to hear about your journey. Share your story with us. Yes, there will be bumps and bruises; that's part of the voyage of being human and being in business.

> WITHOUT CHALLENGE, THERE IS NO ADVENTURE.

Many others will be traveling with you and cheering you on.

Bon Voyage!

Chapter Summary

- ❑ Based on what you've discovered, create a strategy map that guides you to deploy a nimble company.
- ❑ From this map, build an action plan and sequence.
- ❑ Work with your team to deploy your plan.
- ❑ When troubleshooting potential deployment issues, start with mindset.

Ask Yourself

- ❑ Am I willing, able, and ready to lead a nimble company?

❑ Have I made the changes I need to make before I'm able to lead in this new way?

❑ What are my motivations to lead the transformation to a nimble company?

❑ What happens if I choose to maintain the status quo?

❑ What challenges do I foresee leading the nimble transformation?

❑ Where are the mindset, skillset, and toolset gaps in my leadership team's capacities?

❑ What's the path to closing these gaps?

Ask Your Team

❑ How can you help me facilitate our transition to becoming a nimble company?

Action Plan

❑ Create a master plan and deployment path for upleveling your company to Nimbility.

❑ Reach out to NimbilityWorks if you need insight, guidance, or perspective. See page 199 for more information.

❑ Celebrate the successful steps along your path to transforming your team.

❑ Get and read a copy of the companion to this book, *The Nimble C-Suite*, which explores right matching executive temperament to role and lays out a redesign of the executive suite for consistent top performance.

Dedication

We dedicate this book to all the mentors on whose shoulders we stand, and all executives who embrace with all of their minds, hearts, and souls the critical transformation that business must make to realize the better world we all want. You are courageous and we celebrate your heart.

Acknowledgements

We are grateful to our NimbilityWorks cofounders, Mark DiMassimo and Tony Bodoh for their generous, never-ending genius in growing the Nimbility movement.

We recognize and thank the generous, loving people in our life who are our blindspotters and encouragers, sources of inspiration and innovation. In alphabetical order: Sabrina Braham, David Corbin, Mark Hewett, Ed Oakley, Mitch Russo, Chris Stark, Sarah Victory, Rex Wisehart, Bruce Wuollet.

Special thanks for those who provided early input: Mark Hewitt, Douglas Mulhall, and Scott Smith

Mark thanks Molly Smith for her ability to lovingly extract the best of him, even when he resists.

David thanks Laurie Morse for being a magically extraordinary life partner and lightbringer.

And of course, we thank The Divine power that inspired this book and is the Source for much of the content.

This book was outlined and drafted in the inspiring magnificence of Brian Head, UT, and written and edited in peaceful Port St. Joe, FL and shores of San Diego, CA.

About the Authors

Dr. David Gruder, PhD, DCEP, is a clinical and organizational development psychologist, and 12-award-winning bestselling Human Potential Strategist, Business Lifecycle Psychologist, and Culture Architect, who was named America's Integrity Expert by Radio-TV Interview Report.

He has written, contributed to, or been featured, in 25 books, and in Forbes, Inc., Entrepreneur, and Nonprofit Performance magazines, among hundreds of media and podcast interviews. Now in his senior decades, he characterizes himself as a recovering psychologist and professional troublemaker.

David's parents sent him to Woodstock when he was 15 and this experience planted the seeds for his life's mission: to equip leaders and influencers who are called to help repair and evolve the world, with inner, outer and spiritual mindsets and skills to actualize their positive impact.

These days, Dr. Gruder's focus is on catalyzing *Self-Sovereignty That Serves Us All + Governance That Serves Self-Sovereignty*™. He primarily serves Societal Thrival Leaders & Influencers, Middle Market Socially

Responsible Companies, and Integrative Wellbeing Providers, as a trusted advisor, mentor, consultant, trainer, and keynote speaker.

The many hats he currently wears include:

- Integrity Culture Systems™ | Founder and President
- NimbilityWorks™ | Co-Founder & Partner
- NuGen and Lydian Foundation | Co-Founder and Chief Integrity Officer
- Blue Sky Business Resources | Business Lifecycle and M&A Success Psychologist
- Executive Strategy Summits | Executive Development Psychologist
- SynerVision Leadership Foundation™ | Wayfinder, Government Trust Restoration Project Developer, and Principal Trainer
- California Institute for Human Science | Adjunct Faculty
- CEO Space International™ | Legacy Faculty
- ManKind Project | Ritual Elder and Shadow Watcher Training Program Co-Developer and Trainer

He also previously served as Founding President of the Association for Comprehensive Energy Psychology and was an original co-architect and senior trainer for their CEP certification program.

David lives in San Diego, and despite filling all of these roles, he most loves spending plenty of time with his wife Laurie Morse and their two cats.

Also by Dr. David Gruder (Abridged List)

Sensible Self-Help: The First Roadmap for the Healing Journey
The Energy Psychology Desktop Companion

The New IQ: How Integrity Intelligence Serves You, Your Relationships & Our World
The New IQ Workbook: Your Integrity Checkup & Make-over Guide
Conversations With the King: The Enduring Spiritual Legacy of Elvis Presley
Amazing Workplace: Creating the Conditions That Inspire Success (foreword)

And many other publications, training guides, book chapters, forewords, and afterwords.

Website: NimbilityWorks.com and DrGruder.com
LinkedIn: LinkedIn.com/in/Gruder
Twitter: @DavidGruder
Email: Contact@DrGruder.com
Mobile: +1.619.246.1988

Mark S.A. Smith, as a business growth strategist, works with leaders to predictably grow their organization through upgraded executive skills, effective customer acquisition systems, and communication & persuasion strategies.

As an executive coach, executives hire him for strategic coaching, getting unstuck, and use him as a sounding board for developing new, disruptive ideas and choosing new personal and corporate directions.

As co-founder and partner in NimbilityWorks, he brings these skills to clients who must become nimble to thrive in today's chaotic world.

Website: NimbilityWorks.com
LinkedIn: LinkedIn.com/in/MarkSASmith
Twitter: @MarkSASmith
Email: MS@NimbilityWorks.com
Mobile: +1.719.440.0439

Author

Mark wrote seven books and dozens of technology playbooks and sales guides targeting government, educational, healthcare and the private sector and has authored hundreds of articles.

He has also hosted or appeared on hundreds of interviews and podcasts.

Businessman

He has business experience as an electrical engineer, media technologist, computer programmer, hardware salesman, software marketer, and business owner.

Professional Speaker

He speaks at public and corporate events delivering pragmatic ideas to grow and succeed in business. There is no canned speech. He works with you to identify the outcome your group needs and then crafts the presentation to align with your culture, your objectives, and your vision. Contact him for a conversation about speaking at your event.

Builds Business Systems

He designs and implements sales, marketing, and customer acquisition systems that find and recruit willing buyers for disruptive products. He has designed and built channel launch kits, go-to-market playbooks, partner enablement programs, marketing strategy, customer acquisition strategies, executive presentations, systems to up-level business acumen, and more.

Facilitates Executive Strategy Sessions

If you're like many executives in these fast and changing times, you're having challenges clarifying your corporate strategy and getting your executive team all heading the same direction. It's not that your ideas aren't good, the challenge is getting everyone on the same page. Here's a solution.

Using unique, rapid executive decision-making techniques that involve all stakeholders, tapping into the team's personal motivation strategies, and using methods to safely disrupt old ways of thinking, Mark guides your team to get on track and want to stay on track to achieve your goals. And he guarantees it.

Each member of your executive team leaves the event with a "Monday-ready" action plan to deploy with their team to take the correct next steps. You get ongoing support with six months of executive coaching to troubleshoot, encourage, and hold executives accountable for their success.

Mark S.A. Smith facilitates a one and a half to three day on-site executive strategy sessions (timing depends on your mission complexity) with a combination of process training and facilitated conversation about your get-to-market mission.

The deliverables can include:

❑ Discussion of management tools and processes that can be used with your team to accomplish the desired outcome.

❑ Discuss the functions of product, marketing, sales, customer support, operations, finance, and culture in support of the success of this mission.

❑ Discussion of go-to-market processes, selecting the best for your mission based on advanced models.

❑ Clear definition of what success looks like for your mission.

❑ Identify key performance indicators for tracking success and indicating areas which require attention.

❑ Identify resources available to accomplish the mission.

❑ Identify what needs to be accomplished and grounded rationale on doing so.

- ❏ Identify additional resources required to accomplish the mission.
- ❏ Create a corporate messaging and communication plan for socializing and inculcating the mission with key team members.
- ❏ Create a list of prioritized activities and assign responsibility for execution.
  Contact NimbilityWorks to discuss if this is right for your team.

Co-Leads the Executive Nimbility Skills Summit

When you can't work any harder, you must work smarter. Specifically created for profit-and-loss-responsible executives of companies, this 2-day event brings executive skills and insights to founders and staff who have been promoted to the executive suite.

What makes this executive event different is the holistic view of business, not just sales or marketing or leadership, but everything required to operate a sustainable, scalable, profitable, and salable business.

Key outcomes:

- ❏ Develop your executive skill stack — what it is, how it's radically different from a managerial skill stack, and how to intentionally develop it.
- ❏ Gain a deep understanding of the Seven Business Pillars™: Product, Marketing, Sales, Service, Operations, Finance, and Culture, which give you a holistic view of your business to understand the impact of strategy decisions across pillars.
- ❏ Master critical executive business concepts that apply to B2B and B2C, for goods and services, for commercial, non-profit, and governmental operations.

{ 197 }

❑ Develop your own Monday-ready phased plan to improve results and sustainably and profitably grow your company.

❑ Your satisfaction is guaranteed.

This event is co-led with Dr. David Gruder and other guest speakers. Learn more at NimbilityWorks.com/summit

Also by Mark S.A. Smith (Abridged List)

Guerrilla Trade Show Selling with Jay Conrad Levinson & Orvel Ray Wilson

Guerrilla TeleSelling with Jay Conrad Levinson & Orvel Ray Wilson

Guerrilla Negotiating with Jay Conrad Levinson & Orvel Ray Wilson

Linux in the Boardroom

Security in the Boardroom

From MSP to BSP: Pivot to Profit from I.T. Disruption

And many other custom written books and publications for corporate clients.

About NimbilityWorks

NimbilityWorks brings Nimbility to leaders and their teams with a group of extraordinary experts and authors who have a shared, holistic vision of business development and metamorphosis in times of upheaval.

Our big promise: when we choose to work with you, you will become a market leader in three years or less because of the nimbility skills you and your team will acquire.

The NimbilityWorks team blends many decades of direct experience along with essential processes to illuminate paths for seizing your upheavals. Exactly how we work with you depends on your situation and objectives. We will identify specifics during a conversation with you.

NimbilityWorks brings to courageous leaders of challenged organizations a disruptively holistic perspective, processes, and top-level support so that they can lead productive, profitable upheavals in an era of caution, division, confusion, and extraordinary opportunity.

If this resonates with you, you're the Vision Maker who can lead the direction and culture of your team, and you're looking for at least $10 million in growth this year, schedule a 20-minute conversation with the

NimbilityWorks principals. On the introductory call, you'll be talking with:

- ❏ Dr. David Gruder: Develop your executive performance and psychological savvy, undo learned helplessness in your team, and master plan how you will harvest blessings from upheavals.
- ❏ Mark DiMassimo: Make your brand your "unfair" advantage during or because of upheavals. Build and creatively communicate a brand that inspires action with behavior change marketing.
- ❏ Tony Bodoh: Create a culture realignment around customer expectations, to produce ecstatic, loyal customers.
- ❏ Mark S A Smith: Rapid facilitation of complex sales and bringing disruptive products & services to market as fast as possible.

These experts are busy, but they've reserved most Tuesday afternoons 2:30 – 3:30 ET for joint conversations with interested executives. Start this process by speaking with one of our team. Book your time with them here => MeetNimbilityWorks.com

NimbilityWorks Team Industry Expertise

Follows is a partial list of the clients that the NimbilityWorks team members have served along with select validations and endorsements, which illustrate the breadth and depth of our team's perspectives.

Agencies, Marketers, Media and Marketing Technology

- ❏ 5W PR
- ❏ Boost Engagement
- ❏ Brave Thinking Institute

- ❑ CNBC
- ❑ CNN.com
- ❑ Forrester Research
- ❑ IPED
- ❑ Reader's Digest
- ❑ Salesforce
- ❑ Shutterstock
- ❑ SmartMoney
- ❑ The Work Institute
- ❑ Trusted Media Brands

"I've worked for some great agencies during my career. I've also hired many others once I made the move to "the client side." All throughout, I've met a handful of creative leaders who don't just talk the talk, but also dig in and make things happen. Mark (DiMassimo) is at the top of the list. He shows up, dives in head first, gets his team(s) to be well-versed in his clients' business, and creates campaigns which truly do inspire action. It's not just his tagline, it's his DNA. Thus far, I've worked with Mark and his team for two different client engagements and can't wait for round III."

– Phillip Sandler, SVP, Head of Marketing & Growth at **Simulmedia**, SVP, Marketing at **Shutterstock**

"David Gruder is a genius, but more than one: he is 8-in-1. His breadth and depth on multiple subjects is unmatched: leadership, culture, program design & development, integrity, systems & process improvements, wordsmithing, and more. Dr. Gruder is an outstanding lens to amplify and accelerate the impact and difference you are out to make."

– Carl Loop, CEO, **Global Business Builders**

"Before spending a day with David, it had been difficult for me to understand or duplicate the special working chemistry that successful teams have. After spending a day in one of his programs, I now have a far better grasp of quality management structures and dynamics. I see how individuals can be helped to share their unique talents and perspectives in ways that co-create productive cultures that are based on collaboration, integrity and trust. I am not only becoming a better executive due to David's insights and facilitation, but a better man.

    – V. Tyrone Lam, Chief Operating Officer, **GATC Health**

Education
- ❑ Alfred University
- ❑ California Institute for Human Science
- ❑ Great Minds
- ❑ Huntington Learning Centers
- ❑ K-12
- ❑ San Diego County Office of Education Management Academy
- ❑ Hocking College
- ❑ Stride

"Leaders need an integrity check-up and Dr. Gruder is just the man to do it. His simple yet powerful integrity model provides a much-needed shot in the arm."

– Ken Blanchard, Chief Spiritual Officer, **The Ken Blanchard Companies**; Co-author of The One Minute Manager & Leading at a Higher Level

Finance, FinTech, and Financial Media/Education

- ❏ Banker's Healthcare Group
- ❏ CEO Space
- ❏ Citibank
- ❏ Citibank AAdvantage Card
- ❏ Citizens Bank
- ❏ CreditCards.com
- ❏ Everbank/TIAA Bank
- ❏ Forex.com/ Gain Capital
- ❏ IDS/American Express
- ❏ Instinet
- ❏ Investools
- ❏ Online Trading Academy
- ❏ NASDAQ
- ❏ Island ECN
- ❏ MasterCard
- ❏ PMA USA
- ❏ PWC
- ❏ SunTrust
- ❏ TastyTrade
- ❏ ThinkorSwim (now part of TD Ameritrade)
- ❏ TradeStation (Top-Rated Multi-Asset Tech-Forward Brokerage)
- ❏ Voyager (Top Crypto Assets Brokerage App)

"I've always been amazed at Tony's (Bodoh) ability to find creative ways of measuring things and deriving metrics from those measures. He is a constant problem solver. He has a type of insight I have found very rarely in other people. He's great to work with, as well."

– Peter Mancini, Principal Data Scientist, VP, **Citizens Bank**

"Tony (Bodoh) is able to see beyond the tactical and see the possible. He can help you move from current state to desired state with a clear path for success. Through his deep understanding of customer experience, customer journey, and metrics he provides undeniable value to all organizations he helps."

– Jodi L, Director, Decision Science Analytics, Top-ranked Insurance Company

"Tony Bodoh is a never ending treasure chest of knowledge, experience, awareness and thought leadership. If you are one of the fortunate people to work with Tony or through one of his enterprises, you will come away with a huge increase in all areas of life. He truly cares about his clients and their needs. As one of his clients I give him a resounding 5 star rating. He is an absolute pleasure to work with!"

– Kevin Schultz, District Manager, **PMA USA**

"Tony is one of the most dynamic individuals I have ever had the pleasure to meet and work with. His ability to see multiple sides of any situation gives him the unique perspective to provide some of the most effective solutions I have ever seen. The training and experience Tony has puts him heads and shoulders above even the most prominent figures in his industry. Tony is an asset to whoever is fortunate enough to work with him."

– Michael Bloxton, CEO, **Bloxton Investment Group**

Healthcare and Wellness

- ❏ Association for Integrative Health & Medicine
- ❏ Crunch Fitness
- ❏ New York Health & Racket Club
- ❏ HelloFresh
- ❏ FreshDirect
- ❏ CVS Health
- ❏ Dentistry It's Personal
- ❏ Glaxo Smithkline
- ❏ Holistic Healing Heart Center
- ❏ Holistic Mouth Solutions
- ❏ Ideal Image
- ❏ Memorial Sloan-Kettering Cancer Center
- ❏ National Jewish Health
- ❏ Mt. Sinai
- ❏ Rockland County Hospice
- ❏ Merck
- ❏ Oz Crisis Intervention Center
- ❏ PALM Heath
- ❏ Pfizer
- ❏ Restore
- ❏ Sanoviv Hospital
- ❏ U.S. Naval Hospital, 29 Palms
- ❏ UCSD Medical School
- ❏ Vanderbilt University Medical Center
- ❏ White Plains Hospital
- ❏ WW (Weight Watchers Reinvented)
- ❏ Echelon Fitness

"David Gruder is simply a business decathlete and sales genius with a PhD in psychology, like a superman in a cape. Along the way, he has exceeded all of his promises, and generously taught me what Success requires of me. Engaging Dr. David Gruder has been the best move I've ever made in my career.

    – Dr. Felix Liao, DDS, CEO, **Holistic Mouth Solutions**

"Dr. Gruder's work is among the most transformative approaches to business that you will ever see - and he is providing it at a time of the greatest and most uplifting changes in human history."

    – Dr. Mark Hewitt, Founder, **NuGen Development** & the **Lydian Foundation**

Franchise/Services
- Comcast
- Huntington Learning Centers
- Jackson Hewitt
- Online Trading Academy
- Miracle Ear
- Ideal Image
- Vaco (Recruiting services)

"Mark (DiMassimo) has one of the most brilliant minds in the advertising and branding industry. Working with Mark challenged me to think in new and different ways - he's always full of ideas that are creative, engaging, and results-oriented."

    – Kathy Bell, Sr. Director, Corporate Communications, **Comcast**

"Tony (Bodoh) is one of the most forward thinking people I have ever met. His ideas and philosophies on business and strategy are profound and extremely thought provoking. I can say without a doubt that Tony's successes are directly related to not only his way of approaching an issue or problem, but his drive and determination to find a solution."

– Chris Spintzyk, Director, Technology Solutions, **Vaco**

"Tony (Bodoh) was an out-of-the-box thinker who enjoyed solving big problems, many of which related to helping his Gaylord operations and marketing peers improve performance by interpreting the voices of their guests. This demonstration of value ultimately led to a complete redesign of Gaylord's voice-of-the-guest program architecture, and created a new organizational focus on enabling their operations."

– Matt Cohen, Business Development Manager, **Clarabridge**

Manufacturing
- ❑ Encompass Group
- ❑ Fuji
- ❑ Xtracycle

"Mark (S A Smith) uses a proven process that guides executives to rapidly converge on the best strategy to rapidly grow business. When he facilitated with our team, he was able to help us get to breakthrough results faster than ever. We have clarity and an action plan that will get us to our goals and beyond."

– Greg Snoddy, Vice President Healthcare Sales, **Encompass Group** (Industrial Textiles)

"As a CEO, working with Dr. David Gruder really helped improve my leadership effectiveness. Because I'm now equipped with his 'applied integrity and collaboration' skills in areas like commitment, attention to details, and accountability, I've become able to enjoy holding myself to a higher standard, while also helping those I lead and collaborate with do the same. Dr. Gruder's knowledge, training, insight, and wisdom have helped me immeasurably in operating at the highest level in both my business and personal life. I highly recommend utilizing Dr. Gruder, whether you want the corporation you lead to run at a higher level of peak performance, want to significantly upgrade the quality of your work or personal relationships, or want to create sustainable happiness and fulfillment for yourself."

– Brian Hartley, CEO, **The Body Shield, Inc.**

Nonprofits and NGO
- ❏ ManKind Project
- ❏ Meeting Professionals International
- ❏ National Speakers Association
- ❏ Personal Impact Foundation
- ❏ Society of Government Meeting Planners
- ❏ Soldier for Life
- ❏ SouthCentre, Geneva
- ❏ SynerVision Leadership Foundation
- ❏ USO

"Tony Bodoh is amazing. He helped our company uncover valuable information about our clients. The work he performed was PURE GOLD! I highly recommend Tony Bodoh!"
    – John Boggs, CEO, **Brave Thinking Institute**

Real Estate
❏ Bakerson
❏ Exit Real Estate Solutions

Tech
❏ Agilysis
❏ Apple
❏ Arrow Electronics
❏ BEA
❏ Broadcom
❏ CDW
❏ Commvault
❏ ConnectWise
❏ Dell
❏ ePlus
❏ Gateway
❏ GAVS
❏ Hitachi Data Systems
❏ HP
❏ IBM
❏ InfoLink-EXP
❏ Ingram Micro
❏ Insight
❏ Lexmark
❏ Microsoft

- [ ] NASA
- [ ] NetApp
- [ ] Oracle
- [ ] Raytheon
- [ ] Ruckus
- [ ] Samsung
- [ ] Sanmina
- [ ] Sole Solutions Inc
- [ ] Synnex
- [ ] Tech Data
- [ ] Viavi Solutions

"Dr. Gruder provided a high-performance leadership program to our top leaders at Infolink-exp, and I can say that we were all absolutely thrilled with the level of training we got. What made us decide on his program, as opposed to any other, was the fact that he approaches leadership from a perspective of integrity, which is exactly the underlying value that we want to build our company culture around. The program did not disappoint. Our whole team now has an excellent set of practical tools to improve as individuals, to collaborate with each other, and to perform as leaders. I highly recommend Dr. Gruder's program to anyone wanting to provide their team with the tools needed to make quantum leaps in their ability to collaborate and perform at a high level."

– José A. González, CEO, **Infolink-EXP**

"As we spun out the new company, Viavi Solutions, Mark (S A Smith) was a tremendous partner for our team. He leveraged his practical experience and tools for building trusted customer relationships, but also made the effort to truly understand what we were trying to achieve as we established our new brand. The result was a program that helps us arm our global direct and channel sales team, as well as management in all functions, with a simple way to talk about our new company. The program was not only well-received - it was actually used!"

– Susan Schramm, VP Global Sales, and Channel Effectiveness, **VIAVI Solutions** (Test and Measurement)

"During the time I worked with Mark (S A Smith) I have not seen him turn away a challenge. He is one of the most creative business solution-oriented professionals I have met. His ability to quickly understand, analyze and turn problems into executable solutions is well-founded in the experience and personality he brings to the job. I recommend Mark highly to anybody looking for solid business solutions."

– Rene Neumann, Program Director, Global Distributed Channel Management, **IBM**

Travel, Leisure, and Hospitality

- ❑ Avis Budget Group, Budget Rent-a-Car
- ❑ Garza Blanca Residence Club
- ❑ Gaylord Hotels
- ❑ Gaylord Springs Golf Links
- ❑ Grand Ole Opry
- ❑ Gulf Shores & Orange Beach CVB
- ❑ Marriott
- ❑ Quicken Loans Arena
- ❑ Ryman Auditorium

- Starwood Preferred Guest
- American Airlines AAdvantage Program
- Tafer Hotels and Resorts
- The Plaza Hotel
- Millennium Hotels
- Starwood
- Wildhorse Saloon
- Wyndham Garden

"Tony is a master at taking complex situations and breaking them down into manageable components that can easily be made actionable and shared. His communication skills at all levels of the organization are effective and impactful. I wish I had a dozen Tony's on my team!"

– Arthur Keith, General Manager, **Gaylord Opryland Hotel and Convention Center**

"Mark (DiMassimo) has this unique ability to take an award-winning concept from the initial phase to the execution embracing all whom he is working with along the journey as key contributors and stakeholders. He is as generous as he is inspiring. ...Mark has always been instantly available to me by phone, email or text, whenever the need arises for assistance, even knowing that taking my call would have no personal direct benefit. And I didn't even mention his results – top of our class, Platinum Award, and phenomenal growth – and we did it all with ideas and creativity. Marketing Magician!"

– Tom Civitano, Former Director of Sales and Marketing at **The Plaza Hotel**, currently Director of Sales & Marketing at **Stamford Marriott Hotel & Spa**